LARGE-GROUP
PSYCHOLOGY

LARGE-GROUP PSYCHOLOGY

Racism, Societal Divisions, Narcissistic Leaders and Who We Are Now

Vamık D. Volkan

PHOENIX
PUBLISHING HOUSE
firing the mind

First published in 2020 by
Phoenix Publishing House Ltd
62 Bucknell Road
Bicester
Oxfordshire OX26 2DS

British Library Cataloguing in Publication Data

A C.I.P. for this book is available from the British Library

ISBN-13: 978-1-912691-65-4

Typeset by vPrompt eServices Pvt Ltd, India

Printed in the United Kingdom

www.firingthemind.com

This book is dedicated to Elizabeth Volkan, my life partner, who continues to encourage my journey in learning about large groups.

Contents

About the author

Vamık Volkan is an emeritus professor of psychiatry at the University of Virginia and an emeritus training and supervising analyst at the Washington-Baltimore Psychoanalytic Institute. He is the emeritus president of the International Dialogue Initiative and a former president of the Turkish-American Neuropsychiatric Society, the International Society of Political Psychology, the Virginia Psychoanalytic Society, and the American College of Psychoanalysts. He was a member of the International Negotiation Network under the directorship of the former President Jimmy Carter; a member of the Working Group on Terror and Terrorism, International Psychoanalytical Association; a temporary consultant to the World Health Organization in Albania and Macedonia; an inaugural Yitzhak Rabin Fellow, Rabin Center for Israeli Studies, Tel Aviv, Israel; and a Fulbright/Sigmund Freud-Foundation visiting scholar of psychoanalysis in Vienna, Austria.

He is a recipient of the Nevitt Sanford, Elise Hayman, Bryce Boyer, Hans Strupp, Sigmund Freud (given by the city of Vienna) and Mary Sigourney awards and the Margaret Mahler Literature Prize. He was nominated for the Nobel Peace Prize five times; letters of support were sent from twenty-seven countries. Dr. Volkan holds honorary doctorate degrees from Kuopio University (now called the University of Eastern Finland), Finland; Ankara University, Turkey; the Eastern European Psychoanalytic Institute, Russia;

Eastern Mediterranean University, North Cyprus; and Kyrenia - American University, North Cyprus.

Dr. Volkan is the author, coauthor, editor or coeditor of more than fifty psychoanalytic and psychopolitical books, some of which have been translated into Chinese, Finnish, German, Greek, Japanese, Russian, Serbian, Spanish, and Turkish. He has written hundreds of published papers and book chapters. He has served on the editorial boards of sixteen national or international professional journals.

About this book

Charlottesville, Virginia was the home of Thomas Jefferson and James
Monroe, two American presidents. The University of Virginia was founded
in 1819 by Jefferson who is also the principal author of the Declaration of
Independence. I came to Charlottesville in 1963 and became an instructor
at the Department of Psychiatry and Neurology at the University of
Virginia's School of Medicine. During my long tenure at the university,
among several positions I held, I was the medical director of the university's Blue Ridge Hospital for eighteen years. Blue Ridge Hospital was
located next to Monticello, the plantation of Thomas Jefferson which was
designed and built by him. Millions of tourists come to Charlottesville and
visit Monticello which also has slave quarters around the Jefferson mansion.
After my retirement from the University of Virginia's School of Medicine in
2002, Blue Ridge Hospital was closed because the university had built a new
hospital. I have continued to live in Charlottesville.

From August 11 to 12, 2017, a white supremacist rally occurred in my
beautiful city. The ideology of white supremacists in the United States
centers upon establishing a country populated and controlled by pure
descendants of selected white Europeans. Marchers who were from other
locations in the United States chanted racist and anti-Semitic slogans, and
carried Nazi and neo-Nazi symbols as they opposed removing a statue of

Robert E. Lee, a commander of the Confederate States Army during the American Civil War, from Lee Park in the historical downtown. A white supremacist, James Alex Fields Jr., from Ohio, deliberately rammed his car into a gathering of counterprotestors killing thirty-two-year-old Heather Heyer and injuring forty other people.

The morning before these terrible events started, I had left Charlottesville and driven to Washington, DC to fly from Dulles Airport to Berlin, Germany where I would attend a professional meeting and give a talk. When I returned to the United States some days later, news about what had happened in my city and Donald Trump's remarks about "very fine people on both sides," racist neo-Nazis and counterprotestors were being discussed on television again and again.

Our house is at a location surrounded by a forest. I can reach downtown Charlottesville by car within thirty minutes. In April when trees put out new leaves my private environment becomes enveloped with different shades of green. Sitting on my porch I hear the sounds of many birds as well as frogs in a man-made small lake. The only man-made noise that mixes with the sound of nature comes from airplanes when they fly over our house. After I returned from Berlin I could not appreciate or enjoy the beauty of nature. I had to go to downtown and touch places where terrible events had taken place and where Heather Heyer, whom I did not know, was murdered.

What had happened in Charlottesville made me think about my life in the United States, starting in 1957 as a voluntary immigrant, my personal observations and experiences of racism, anti-Semitic and anti-Muslim sentiments as well as positive aspects of "American exceptionalism." I wanted to write a book about my observations on the political division in the United States. I considered the American white supremacist movement as a "large group" with its own subdivisions. My term "large group" describes hundreds, thousands, or millions of people—most of whom will never see or even know about each other as individuals, but who share many of the same sentiments. Already I had written several books and many papers describing ethnic, national, religious, and ideological large-group problems. Because of this I hesitated to start working on a new book.

On December 7, 2018, James Alex Fields Jr. was found guilty of first-degree murder and eight counts of malicious wounding. People, including survivors, who were gathered outside the courtroom marched in the streets of downtown Charlottesville expressing their relief. I was told that an African-American woman and her African-American husband were with Heather Heyer when she was hit by the murderer's car. This African-American gentleman was a witness during the trial. Some months later, I learned that, after the trial, members of the church where his wife's family attends services were threatened by white supremacists.

Little more than three months later new attacks on mosques, churches, and synagogues occurred in different parts of the world. On March 15, 2019, a white supremacist killed many people in the Al Noor mosque during Friday prayers at the Linwood Islamic Centre in Christchurch, New Zealand. Donald Trump attributed this tragedy and similar ones to acts of "a small group of people that have very, very serious problems." This was a simplistic way of looking at what is happening in the present world. The next month many suspects were arrested after a series of church and hotel bombings on Easter Sunday in Sri Lanka, killing 253 persons and wounding 450 others. On April 27, 2019, a shooting in a synagogue near San Diego, California, dominated the news and John T. Earnest, only nineteen years old, was arrested on suspicion of murder and attempted murder. It was suspected that, before he was arrested, he had set a fire at a San Diego county mosque. Two weeks later a fire broke out in the Diyanet Mosque in New Haven, Connecticut. No one was harmed. The authorities believe that the fire was set intentionally.

During late spring 2019, I went to Warsaw as a guest of the Polish Psychoanalytic Society. Members of this society and other mental health workers wanted to explore how they could express their professional opinions about the totalitarianism and paranoia in their country. The governing Law and Justice Party in Poland was against the European Union's promoting a secular vision for the continent. According to the party such a vision would be at odds with the Polish identity. The leaders of the party were also demonizing gays and lesbians as a threat to Poland's soul. The Law and Justice Party greatly benefits from the support of the Catholic Church. Almost 40 percent of the population attends Mass weekly. Church sermons and the Catholic media strongly support the governing party. The board members of the Polish Psychoanalytic Society wanted me to make a presentation at the society's May 18, 2019 meeting and focus on the psychological understanding of political and societal divisions in a national large group.

When I was in Warsaw, the two-hour documentary, "Tell No One," by journalist Tomasz Sekielski and his brother Marek Sekielski, was viewed on YouTube over 18 million times within a couple of days, exposing widespread child sexual abuse by Polish priests. Such scandals have been known in the United States, the United Kingdom, Australia, and elsewhere.

Now it shook up the population in Poland. One of the abuser priests was identified as the personal chaplain of Lech Walesa, a Nobel Peace Prize winner who had served as president of Poland from 1990 to 1995. The Polish people began to wonder if this documentary would make an impact on the power of the ruling party.

When I returned to the USA after spending a short time in Poland, news about the struggle regarding Brexit in the United Kingdom, elections in India where minorities—from Muslims and Christians to lower castes and liberals—were under pressure, and the possibility of starting an impeachment process against Donald Trump provided other examples of societal divisions. In many countries people are busy asking a metaphorical question, "Who are we now?" and coming up with seemingly opposite answers. My motivation to write a new book and update my findings on large-group psychology returned. I also wanted a chance to describe my *personal observations and experiences* related to this topic.

This book provides a summary of Sigmund Freud's ideas about large groups. Generally speaking, his and many of his followers' main focus was to study what a large group means for an individual. I explain what is large-group psychology *in its own right*. This means making formulations about the conscious and unconscious shared past and present historical/ psychological experiences that exist within a large group. Making such formulations enlarges our understanding of the emergence of present-day societal–political–religious events, leader–follower relationships, and allows us to look at the interactions between opposing large groups in depth. This is similar to a psychoanalyst making formulations about his or her analysands' developmental histories associated with various conscious and unconscious fantasies in order to understand what motivates certain behavior patterns, symptoms, and habitual interpersonal relationships.

In this book I describe how a child becomes a member of a large group and how adults sometimes develop a second type of large-group identity. Looking at such phenomena provides background data for an examination of the spread of the metaphorical question, "Who are we now?", racism, authoritarian regimes, malignant political propaganda, wall building, and interferences with democratic processes and human rights issues. I wish to raise the need to examine the present world affairs also from a psychological angle. I will not use many technical psychoanalytic terms, in order to address a wider audience.

CHAPTER ONE

Personal motivations for studying large-group psychology

Traditionally psychoanalysts do not write about their own motivations for studying selected issues of human psychology. Such motivations may remain unconscious. If psychoanalysts are aware of events starting in their childhood which directed them to be preoccupied with a psychological topic or to seek individuals who share specific types of traumas and behavior patterns to treat, they do not wish to publicize and make this knowledge available for their analysands.

Stanley Olinick (1980) wondered about what motivates a mental health worker to become a psychoanalyst. He stated that such a powerful motivation is "the genetic effect of a rescue fantasy having to do with a depressive mother, the latter having induced such rescue fantasy in her receptive child." He added that for such relatedness of mother and child to be formative, "it must be early, though the necessary duration is not clear" (Olinick, 1980, pp. 12–13). Olinick did not include information about his own life.

Joseph Reppen (1985) was curious to know how other psychoanalysts conduct an analysis, what informs their thinking and methods, and what their motivations are. He asked ten American and two European psychoanalysts to speak to others with openness and candor about their work. These twelve psychoanalysts' contributions were published. His book illustrated, as Reppen stated, how broad the Freudian perspective can be, and how deeply personal is the work of a psychoanalyst. Looking at Reppen's book recently, however, I noted that the twelve contributors primarily described their methods and techniques without providing detailed samples of events in their lives which had influenced their professional activities. I was one of the twelve psychoanalysts.

At the present time I feel freer to share more information about my background because I stopped my clinical practice in 2000. Since then I have continued supervising or consulting with younger psycho-analysts from several countries. My work as a supervisor led me to notice many supervisees' emotional attachment to or avoidance of working on certain psychological issues. As I was not their therapist, I would not explore why they illustrated excitement or hesitation about working on certain human problems. Some of them volunteered to tell me their understanding of how certain events in their own lives and in their countries, in spite of their going through personal analyses, had continued to influence them in liking or avoiding what to examine. In this chapter I will report events from my childhood which played a role in my becoming a psychoanalyst, spending decades in examining international conflicts and traumas away from my couch, and evolving large-group psychology in its own right.

Cyprus, a Mediterranean island, is known as the birthplace of Aphrodite, the Ancient Greek goddess of love. It was well populated during the Neolithic (or "new stone") Age during the period 4000 to 3000 BC. The island has been a hotly contested prize since 1500 BC because of its strategic location off the coast of Asia Minor and rich deposits of ore. The word *copper* is said to be derived from the name of *Cyprus*. Mycenean settlers colonized the island and Phoenicians and Achaean Greeks set up independent city states there. The island was dominated by a long series of conquerors—Egyptians, Persians, Macedonians, Romans, Byzantines, Arabs, the Crusaders, the Frankish kings, the Genoese, Venetians, and the Ottoman Turks. Then, it became a British colony before the establishment of the Republic of Cyprus in 1960.

I was born to Cypriot Turkish parents in 1932 when the island was a British colony. A year earlier there were 347,959 souls on the island (Luke, 1952). Two ethnic groups, Christian Greeks and in lesser numbers Muslim Turks lived next door to each other in the same cities, towns, and some villages. In other villages only Greeks or Turks lived. There were also smaller numbers of Armenians, Maronites, and Phoenicians on the island. As I was growing up in Nicosia, the capital city of the island, I would meet

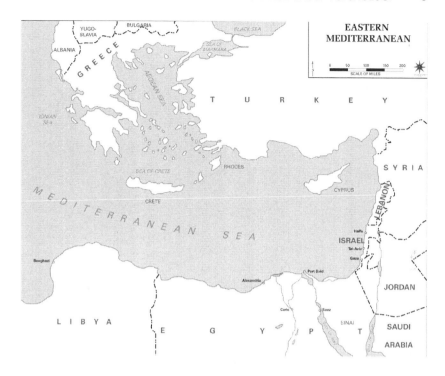

Cypriot Greeks and Cypriot Armenians in my neighborhood, in market places, near churches or mosques, and in other locations every day. I would also see people from Great Britain. The headmaster of my Turkish high school was an Englishman, and his wife was Armenian. The British on the island belonged to the "ruling" class, the rest of us were "natives." As I grew older and became aware of the impact of history on human psychology, I started to realize why Greeks and Turks, as "natives," invested so much in their Greekness and Turkishness in order to support their self-esteem and link themselves to their respective "motherlands," Greece and Turkey. I learned that during the year before I was born the Cypriot Greeks had revolted against the British, sought *Enosis* (union) with Greece.

When I was a child, I became aware of the concept of "enemy," but the British people were not the "enemy." After the Nazis' 1941 airborne invasion of another Mediterranean island, Crete, it was expected that they would next invade Cyprus. My father had already hired someone to dig an underground bunker in our garden. We took refuge there on many occasions, even in the middle of rainy nights after sirens woke us. Sometimes bombs were dropped on the island from German and Italian military airplanes. We would wait in the bunker for the all-clear siren to inform us that the danger had passed. Food was rationed and we were forced to eat dark, tasteless bread and taught how to wear gas masks. Germans and Italians were the "enemy." During World War II an estimated 35,000 Cypriot volunteers, both Greek and Turkish, served side by side in the British armed forces—650 died, 2,500 were taken prisoner.

As the war was going on, I began noticing people belonging to another large-group identity. Indian Sikh soldiers with long beards and turbans were walking around the streets of my neighborhood. I witnessed a British Spitfire shooting down an Italian war plane just above my elementary schoolyard where I was playing with other kids. This must have been a frightening experience for me because I kept a small piece of glass from the plane's wreckage for decades. By keeping it, and in a sense controlling it, most likely I was attempting to master my childhood anxiety that I might lose my life. The Germans never did invade Cyprus.

Cypriot Greeks and Cypriot Turks went to separate schools. There was only one "English school" for both Greek and Turkish teenagers to enroll in. After I finished the Turkish high school on the island I went to Turkey for my medical education. I graduated in 1956 and six months later I took part in a process which was called the "brain drain." The United States lacked medical doctors at this time and therefore attracted physicians from around the world. My arrival in America as a young physician coincided with new large-group conflicts on Cyprus. The Cypriot Greeks, with a desire to unite Cyprus with Greece, began to attack the United Kingdom's forces and civilians, as well as to oppress Cypriot Turks. Reliance on terrorism would become routine.

During my last two years of medical school in Turkey I shared a rented room with Erol Mulla, another Cypriot Turkish medical student who was two years younger than me, and he became the brother I never had. Several months after my arrival in the United States I received a letter from my father. In the envelope there was a newspaper notice with Erol's picture describing how my friend had gone to Cyprus from Turkey to visit his ailing mother. While trying to purchase medicine for her at a pharmacy he was shot seven times by a Cypriot Greek terrorist. This person killed Erol, a bright young man with a promising future, in order to terrorize the ethnic group to which he belonged. Erol was killed in the name of large-group identity. During my first year in the United States I was an intern in a Chicago hospital, in a new environment with no friends. I could not mourn Erol's death.

Following my medical internship in Chicago I went to Chapel Hill, North Carolina and completed my training in psychiatry at the North Carolina University Hospital. After spending five years in North Carolina I came to Charlottesville, Virginia and also became a United States citizen. Now, I was a "voluntary immigrant." I lived in safety while my family and friends in Cyprus were living in enclaves in subhuman conditions surrounded by Cypriot Greeks. At that time, I had no names for my complicated mourning and survival guilt. After settling in Charlottesville, I started my personal analysis and psychoanalytic training by travelling from Charlottesville to Washington, DC for some years.

While studying medicine in Turkey I knew that I wanted to be a psychiatrist and a psychoanalyst. Much later I realized one important factor leading me to have such a wish. When I was a youngster, we did not have a typical library in our rented house in Nicosia. In those days middle-class families did not have electricity in their houses even when they were living in cities or big towns. I was in my mid-teens before I could start to read and do my school homework during evenings without the need of an oil lamp. My father, an elementary school master, kept his books in a huge black wooden box in my parents' bedroom. One day, as World War II was going on, I realized that this huge box was locked. My two older sisters told me that my father had obtained a German dictionary so he would be able to communicate with the Nazis if they were to invade Cyprus and protect his family. They also informed me that this was a forbidden act, so our father had to hide his German dictionary. I recall developing an interest in this box and trying to open it when no one was around. Psychoanalysts easily may imagine that my preoccupation with this locked box was related to a young boy's oedipal issues, his curiosity about sexual secrets in a parental bedroom. One day I managed to open the box and found the German dictionary. Next to it there was another book, Sigmund Freud's *Three Essays on the Theory of Sexuality* (1905d) in Turkish. I thought that my father was not only hiding the dictionary, he was also keeping his young son from knowing sexual topics. Later I would learn who Sigmund Freud was. I think that this story tells how I became interested in psychoanalysis.

The year I was born Albert Einstein was fifty-three years old and Sigmund Freud was seventy-six. The following year, in 1933, Einstein who was then living in France and was the honorary president of the

Organization for the Protection of Jewish Population (OZE) wrote a letter to the president of the Cabinet of Ministers of Turkey. In this letter he asked the Turkish authorities "to allow forty professors and doctors from Germany to continue their scientific and medical work in Turkey. The above mentioned cannot practice further in Germany on account of the laws governing there now. The majority of these men possess vast experience, knowledge and scientific merits and could prove very useful when settling in a new country." OZE would pay their salaries during the

UNION DES SOCIÉTÉS "OSE"
POUR LA PROTECTION DE LA SANTÉ
DES POPULATIONS JUIVES

COMITÉ D'HONNEUR

Prof. A. EINSTEIN, *Président.*
Prof. A. BESREDKA, *Vice-Président - Paris.*
Prof. RADCLIFFE N. SALAMAN, *V.-Président - Londres*

SOCIÉTÉS AFFILIÉES

ALLEMAGNE.
ANGLETERRE.
DANTZIG.
ÉTATS-UNIS.
LETTONIE.
LITHUANIE.
POLOGNE (T. O. Z.)
ROUMANIE.

אָ זָ ע "י

פֿאַרבאַנד פֿון די געזעלשאפֿטן
פֿאַרן ייִדישן געזונטשוץ

TÉL.:

PARIS (XVII), LE 17 September, 1933
4, Rue Roussel

T. C.
BAŞBAKANLIK
CUMHURİYET ARŞIVI

Your Excellency,

As Honorary President of the World Union "OZE" I beg to apply to Your Excellency to allow forty professors and doctors from Germany to continue their scientific and medical work in Turkey. The above mentioned cannot practise further in Germany on account of the laws governing there now. The majority of these men possess vast experience, knowledge and scientific merits and could prove very useful when settling in a new country.

Out of a great number of applicants our Union has chosen fourty experienced specialists and prominent scholars, and is herewith applying to Your Excellency to permit these men to settle and practise in your country. These scientists are willing to work for a year without any remuneration in any of your institutions, according to the orders of your Government.

In supporting this application, I take the liberty to express my hope, that in granting this request your Government will not only perform an act of high humanity, but will also bring profit to your own country.

I have the honour to be,

Your Excellency's obedient servant,

(Prof. Albert Einstein)

His Excellency
The President of the Cabinet of Ministers
of the Turkish Republic.

5

first year of their stay in Turkey. The letter ends as follows: "In supporting this application, I take the liberty to express my hope, that in granting this request your Government will not only perform an act of high humanity, but will also bring profit to your own country."

Einstein's request was sent to the Turkish Ministry of Education, which rejected this proposal on the grounds that there were no existing conditions to accept such an unusual request. But Einstein's request was accepted when the leader of new Turkey, Mustafa Kemal, who would become better known as Atatürk, intervened. At that time the Turkish Republic, born from the ashes of the Ottoman Empire, was only ten years old and extremely poor, but had accepted some German-Jewish scholars to come to Turkey even before Einstein's request. Following Einstein's letter, in 1933, thirty German-Jewish scholars and their families came to Turkey, and eventually 190 other intellectuals and their families arrived. Thus, ultimately, over 1,000 lives were saved (Reisman, 2006). Years later when I was a medical student at the University of Ankara some of the German-Jewish professors who had escaped to Turkey after Einstein's letter was written were still teaching medicine. This is how, for the first time in my life, I met people who were Jewish, members of another large group who were directly or indirectly victimized by the Nazis.

In 1959, negotiations in which the United Kingdom, Greece, and Turkey took part led to the establishment during the following year of the Republic of Cyprus, with a Cypriot Greek president and a Cypriot Turkish vice-president, each elected for a five-year term. British colonial rule ended. A cabinet was formed, composed of seven Greek and three Turkish members, and the same 70–30 ratio was to be maintained in Parliament and in all branches of the civil service. As I stated above, before December 1963 the Turks on Cyprus were interspersed among the Greek majority. On December 21, 1963, violence erupted. Over two days, up to 133 Turkish Cypriots were killed by Greek Cypriots in what became known by Turkish Cypriots as the "Bloody Christmas Massacre." During Bloody Christmas, 8,667 Cypriot Turks abandoned 103 villages to take refuge in six enclaves where Turks were forced to live surrounded by their enemies. Twenty-five or thirty thousand Cypriot Turks would become internally displaced people between December 1963 and the summer of 1964. During this time the Turkish side lost 364 persons and 174 Greeks were also killed. Each side brought charges of atrocity against the other. For the first five years, the Turks were not allowed out of their surrounded enclaves, occupying only 3 percent of the island, and were in a sense imprisoned. A single home might shelter more than ten families from time to time. Internally displaced Cypriot Turks not fortunate enough to join relatives lived in caves or tents. After five years had passed, they were allowed to move from one surrounded enclave to another, and to pass through the Greek sectors, experiencing humiliation, as long as they returned to their ghettos.

Cypriot Turks did not experience "freedom" until the Turkish forces landed on the island on July 20, 1974. After fierce battles the Turkish military cut the island in two, creating northern Turkish and southern Greek sides. According to the Greek sources 6,000 Greeks were killed and 3,000 were missing (Markides, 1977). Turkish sources gave their losses as 1,500 dead and 2,000 wounded. Some 160,000 Cypriot Greeks were forced into the southern part of the island, and 60,000 Cypriot Turks who had been living in the south escaped north as voluntary refugees. Many individuals from both sides were severely traumatized. Today the island remains divided between Cypriot Turks in the North and Cypriot Greeks in the South.

When I was training to become a psychiatrist in Chapel Hill, my main mentor, Wilfred Abse, was a Jewish professor who had come to the United

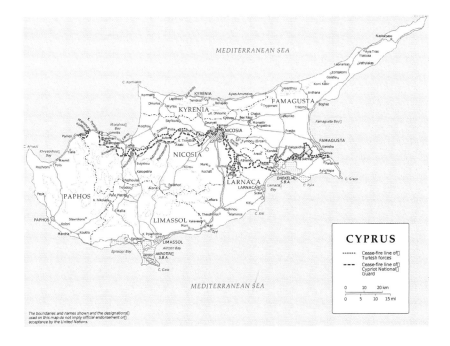

States from Great Britain. He was not directly affected by the Holocaust, and I do not recall talking with him about Jewish history. The first big emotional impact the Nazis' treatment of the Jewish people had on me occurred when I was in Chapel Hill and treating a young man in the inpatient unit. He was complaining of marital problems and exhibiting depression. He would cry during his sessions with me. I could see him crying intensely, but I would not hear him. It was very peculiar to observe someone crying so hard in silence. Slowly I learned that his family had hidden in the attic of a house belonging to a Christian family at a location in Europe occupied by the Nazis. As an infant he had to sleep in a drawer of an old chest. One day, Nazi soldiers came to the house looking for hidden Jewish people. When the baby started to cry, his father put his hand over the infant's mouth, afraid that the Nazi soldiers would hear his son's crying. Of course, my patient as an adult did not remember this incident, but while he was growing up the family would refer to it again and again. I sensed that the father had experienced a great deal of guilt and shame for silencing his baby for the sake of saving himself and his wife. Working with this young man connected me emotionally to the history of the Holocaust.

My analysis and my psychoanalytic training took place when my family and friends on the island were living in a surrounded enclave in Nicosia. In the United States there was not much information about their horrible experiences. My analyst whom I liked very much and who had a great professional reputation was Jewish. I recall wondering if his family also had experienced horrible traumas. Decades later I wondered why during my analysis we did not examine my family members' living in an enclave in Cyprus surrounded by their enemies and the emotional impact of their suffering on me. Was my analyst not paying attention to external events by following a classical analytic methodology? Or, did he avoid remembering societal cruelty by not paying attention to events in Cyprus?

In my mind I was picturing my family members and friends living in surrounded enclaves like Jews in concentration camps. However, I was embarrassed to express such a thought since the Holocaust was an unbelievably huge tragedy and it should not be compared with the victimization of a small group people who had a "mother country" nearby which, they hoped, would save them. Only years later, after my psychoanalysis was over, I realized how I had found ways to deal with my emotional loneliness. Here are two examples: The first example is my unconsciously choosing the topic of complicated mourning as my initial clinical research (Volkan, 1972, 1981). The second one was my developing a special relationship with psychoanalyst William Niederland whose main contribution to the literature was on survival guilt (Niederland, 1961, 1968). Then, I had an unusual chance to study large groups in conflict and, in a sense, developed a new career.

On November 19, 1977, Egyptian president Anwar Sadat came to Israel, visited the Knesset, and famously referred to a "psychological wall" between the Israelis and the Arabs—a wall that, he stated, accounted for 70 percent of the problems between them. In response, the American Psychiatric Association's Committee on Psychiatry and Foreign Affairs, of which I was a member, brought influential Arabs and Israelis together for unofficial dialogues for six years to find out if this "wall" could be made permeable. Following this experience, I opened the Center for the Study of Mind and Human Interaction (CSMHI) at the University of Virginia School of Medicine with a faculty of psychoanalysts, other mental health professionals, former diplomats, political scientists, historians, an environmentalist, and a linguist. A psychoanalyst can be effective, as Alexander Mitscherlich (1971) indicated, when he or she learns to work as a member of an interdisciplinary team. My interdisciplinary CSMHI team and I visited many areas of the world where international conflicts existed and brought together representatives of opposing large groups, such as Soviets and Americans, Russians and Estonians, Croats and Bosnians, Georgians and South Ossetians, Turks and Greeks, for years-long unofficial dialogues. Taking a "trip" with a patient into her internal world while sitting behind the therapeutic couch is one thing; settling down between enemy representatives who sometimes were hurling fiercely aggressive sentiments at one another or standing among massively traumatized persons in situations of real and imminent danger, was quite another. Our methodology for "unofficial diplomacy" became known as the "Tree Model" (Volkan, 1997, 1999a, 2006). I chose a Greek-American psychiatrist, Demetrios Julius, as my assistant director during these activities. He remains one of my best friends.

I also studied traumatized societies such as Albania and Romania after the fall of its dictators, Enver Hoxha and Nicolae Ceauşescu respectively, and Kuwait after the invasion by Saddam Hussein's forces (Volkan, 1988, 1997, 2004, 2006). I became a member of the International Negotiation

Network (INN) under the directorship of former President Jimmy Carter for more than a decade, starting in 1989. Besides Jimmy Carter, I met well-known political or societal leaders such as Mikhail Gorbachev, Yasser Arafat, Arnold Rüütel, and Desmond Tutu, and spent some time with them. The first president of North Cyprus, Rauf Denktaş, was a friend of mine.

CSMHI applied a growing theoretical and field-proven base of knowledge to issues such as ethnic tension, racism, national identity, terrorism, societal trauma, transgenerational transmissions, leader–follower relationships, and other aspects of national and international conflict. Psychoanalytic training does not make someone an expert political analyst. My new career at CSMHI gave me the opportunity to develop large-group psychology in its own right (Volkan, 2013). CSMHI was closed in 2005, three years after I retired from the University of Virginia.

In 2018, I established the International Dialogue Initiative (IDI). IDI is a private, multidisciplinary group comprised of psychoanalysts, academics, diplomats, business people, and other professionals from eight countries who meet biannually to bring a psychologically informed perspective to the study and amelioration of social conflict. I will tell more about the IDI later in this book.

Before summarizing Freud's writings on large-group psychology, referring to other colleagues' works, and describing my concepts illustrating large-group psychology I will add two more stories from my childhood which I believe also motivated me to study this topic.

The first story refers to my being a "replacement child," that is, one whose mother or mothering person unconsciously deposits the image of a lost person into his or her developing self-representation. Important adults perceive and relate to the newborn baby, to some degree or other, as the child's already dead sibling or another lost important individual and give the replacement child certain psychological tasks (Ainslie & Solyom, 1986; Cain & Cain, 1964; Green & Solnit, 1964; Legg & Sherick, 1976; Poznanski, 1972; Volkan & Ast, 1997). Such processes mostly are carried out unconsciously.

I fully realized being a replacement child after my personal analysis was over. The story of my being a replacement child was linked to a political agreement between two large groups, the Ottoman Empire and the United Kingdom, which would make a dramatic change in the history of Cyprus.

In 1571 Cyprus became an Ottoman territory. More than 300 years later, in 1878, the Ottoman Sultan Abdül Hamid transferred Cyprus to the United Kingdom on a temporary basis in order to receive British support in the conflict between the Ottomans and Russians. In turn the UK would pay 100,000 pounds for this privilege (Simmons, 2015). During World War I the Ottomans joined the Central powers. Then the British declared complete annexation of Cyprus into the British Empire. After the collapse of the Ottoman Empire the new Turkish Republic confirmed the UK's annexation of Cyprus. Without a war on the island Cyprus became a British colony.

When I was growing up my mother sometimes would tell her children that her side of the family originally was from Bursa, the first capital of the Ottoman Empire before they conquered Constantinople (Istanbul) in 1453 and made that city their capital. I have no evidence of this belief. There is information, however, about my family on my mother's side going back five generations before me. My mother's grandfather's grandfather was named Mehmet. People referred to him as Hacı Mehmet. "Hacı" is derived from the Arabic "ḥājj." This title is given to Muslim individuals who had gone to Mecca, the most holy place for Muslims. In Islam it is mandatory for a Muslim to visit Mecca at least one time if he or she is physically and financially able to make the pilgrimage. Hacı Mehmet also had another title, Hesapker (a person dealing with finances). According to my mother he was in charge of the financial administration of the Ottoman Cyprus. Again, I have no proof about this, but as a child I imagined that my mother's family belonged to the Ottoman elite. Hacı Mehmet's grandson, my mother's grandfather, was named Ömer Vamık. We know that he was the kadı (religious judge) of Nicosia. His wife was his relative and also had Hesapker ancestors. They lived in the Ömerge district of Nicosia. The family was rich; they had fourteen stores, including a jewelry shop. Today the Ömerge district is in the Greek section of Nicosia after the capital city was divided between Greeks and Turks in 1974.

My mother's grandfather would become the last Ottoman kadı in Nicosia. After the Ottoman Sultan "rented" the island to the British and a British governor and his people became the administrators of the island in 1878, Ömer Vamık was removed from his prestigious position and was sent to a village about thirty miles away near the town of Lefke. I suspect that the British assigned him to carry out some religious/legal business at this village and in Lefke. His wife Zehra would not leave Nicosia to join her husband. In those days thirty miles was a long distance between a husband and wife. At the new location, my mother's grandfather married another woman. Muslims could have up to four wives. When I was growing up, I knew that I had relatives in Lefke due to Ömer Vamık's second marriage. I would not meet them until I was an adult. It was as if we were the original and "good" descendants of *Kadı* Ömer Vamık and those in Lefke did not count.

I suspect that my mother's father, the son of *Kadı* Ömer Vamık, was angry with his father. He did not work and lived off the family's money. His wife, my grandmother was also a descendant of *Hesapker* Mehmet. The family began losing its wealth and prestige. Eventually the family stores would be gone. After I went through my personal analysis, I slowly began to realize how my mother had certain behavior patterns that indicated her trying to hold on to the family's past glories. For example, she declared a condition for marrying my father, a villager: she would never wash dirty clothes. And, after she married my father, she did not wash clothes even though they had a limited amount of money for hiring help. My mother's other belief was that our family members should be educated and have prestigious jobs. She became an elementary school teacher. At that time, this was a very unusual thing for a Muslim woman to accomplish. The British would not allow a married woman to remain as a teacher. So, my mother, after her engagement to my father, told her future husband to wait for three years before they would get married. She wanted to teach for at least three years and be known as an educated woman.

My mother, the oldest child, had three siblings, all boys. The next sibling to my mother was named after his *Kadı* grandfather, Ömer Vamık. After finishing high school my mother's siblings went to Turkey for further education. My uncle Ömer Vamık, while studying engineering in Istanbul went missing for fifty-three days. Then his body was found in the Sea of Marmara. I would be born five years later and named after him and become the new living Ömer Vamık.

Earlier I referred to Stanley Olinick's (1980) idea that a depressive mother induces rescue fantasies in a receptive child, and this is a powerful motivation for the child to become a psychoanalyst in the future. When I was growing up, on the anniversary of my uncle Ömer Vamık's death, my grandmother and mother would bring out his photographs and some items, such as a shirt or school book, that had belonged to my dead uncle from a dark room where they were kept. They would touch these photographs and items and cry. My mother and grandmother were not depressed. But they experienced an unending mourning. They would tell me how my uncle was an extremely smart and intelligent person. He was always number one in his class. I do recall having examined my uncle's photographs and having compared his appearance with my own. I was fascinated by the notion of a likeness.

My mother and grandmother believed in a fantasy that some of my uncle's classmates at the engineering school were very jealous of my most brilliant uncle and because of this, they killed him. There was picture of my dead uncle with his six friends. As I was growing up, I used to fantasize that these six individuals were my uncle's murderers. I learned from an older sister that our grandfather had sought the aid of a psychic to solve the mystery of his son's death and had been told by the psychic that his son had been murdered by "six friends." No one even imagined that my uncle might have committed suicide. Perhaps the pressure on him to excel and bring back the family's glory might have had a role in his losing his life.

Years later, after I became a psychoanalyst, I realized that I was a "replacement child." I replaced my dead uncle and then owned the psychological task to repair *Kadı* Ömer Vamık and his family's image which was traumatized by a historical event, a political agreement by the authorities of two large groups.

My second story is my being kidnapped by a Cypriot Greek woman when I was less than two years old. I have no memory of this event. But my mother, my two older sisters, and my grandmother used to tell the story of this event, with some anxiety, again and again when I was growing up. Apparently, at the time of this kidnapping the family still lived in the Ömerge district, but in a rented house. My mother had put me into a baby carriage as she, my grandmother, my two sisters, and I were leaving the house for an outing. I was left at the front door which was open when everybody went back inside the house to retrieve something. When they returned to the front door the baby carriage was empty. Panic set in when they realized that I was gone. My mother started screaming. Neighbors, both Turkish and Greek, joined together to search for me in the neighborhood. At the end of the day I was found at the electricity generator of Nicosia. My understanding was that my kidnapper, the Greek woman, had mental difficulties. She found me "cute," and stole me with the idea of having a child to raise. I recall that while hearing this story again and again when I was growing up, I would focus on being liked and wanted by this Greek woman. Most likely I would do so in order not to feel the adults' anxiety. Now I realize how my childhood fantasy of being wanted by a person from another ethnic group must have played a role in my involvement in making peace between opposing large groups.

My being born in Cyprus, experiencing relationships between different large groups, my childhood fear of Nazis, and other stories as recounted here, served as a living laboratory for my involvement in large-group conflicts and my work on large-group psychology in its own right (Atik, 2019).

CHAPTER TWO

Large-group psychology
in its own right

Sigmund Freud published his paper *Group Psychology and the Analysis of the Ego* in 1921. He did not consider mere collections of people as a group and described race, nation, religious or professional organizations as groups. Following Gustave Le Bon's (1895) ideas on group mind Freud's focus was on how individuals in a group develop new experiences such as losing distinctiveness and being subject to suggestions. He compared the Church and the army. While these two groups are different in many aspects each has a head (Jesus Christ and commander-in-chief) who rules and treats all the individuals with equal love. The members of a group idealize the leader as they, in Freud's terms, "put one and the same object in the place of their ego ideal" and identify "themselves with one another in their ego (1921c, p. 116).

In an earlier paper Freud (1912–13) described totemism and incest taboo by making reference to prehistoric times and the idea of the "primal horde" which in reality has never been observed. In *Group Psychology and the Analysis of the Ego* he linked group formation to the "primal horde" and wrote about the leader of the group being a "primal father." The primal father prevents his sons from satisfying their sexual impulses. Only the successor will have the possibility of sexual satisfaction. It is clear that Freud's interest was what a group means for an individual and how an individual behaves as a member of a group. If mutual ties cease to exist panic starts. Freud also pointed out how belonging to a group creates prejudice toward strangers.

It was Robert Waelder (1936) who first stated that Freud was describing regressed large groups. I will examine large-group regression at the end of this chapter.

Starting with Sigmund Freud, some psychoanalysts have been interested in large-group psychology. However, their focus, like Freud's, primarily was on what a large group means to an individual, such as an oedipal father. Following the realization that a child's mind does not evolve without his or her interactions with the mother and/or a mothering person, some authors postulated that members experience their large group as a maternal ego ideal or a breast-mother who repairs narcissistic injuries. (For example, see: Anzieu, 1971, 1984; Chasseguet-Smirgel, 1984; Kernberg, 1989, 2003a, 2003b). It was primarily group analysts who focused more on the importance of social–cultural sources in patterns of anxiety in group mind (Foulkes, 1973; Hopper & Weinberg, 2011; Pines & Lipgar, 2002). Robi Friedman (2008) stated that persons and their groupings are interrelated and added that dreaming is both a cocreation of mind and society and cocreator of them.

In the literature the terms "group" or "large group" continue to refer to various situations. For example, these terms are used for people who come together for therapy or individuals from different ethnic backgrounds who meet to discuss differences between them or for members of a professional organization or nation. In the introduction to this book I stated what I mean by the term "large group" and what is large-group psychology *in its own right*.

In this chapter I will describe concepts related to large-group psychology in its own right and give examples illustrating these concepts. These examples come from different countries and locations.

In the past, when I described traumatizing aggressive events initiated by large groups, on some occasions, I received feedback from colleagues who were members of these large groups expressing their disappointment in me. They had felt that I was deliberately making humiliating remarks about their ethnic or national identities. For example, after I studied and wrote about what happened in Serbia under the leadership of Slobodan Milošević (Volkan 1996, 1997) a colleague in Serbia kept accusing me of being an enemy of the Serbian people because of my Turkish background. I was involved in bringing together influential representatives of Turkish intelligence, Turkish military, and influential people of Kurdish origin in Turkey, including a close associate of Abdullah Öcalan, the imprisoned leader of PKK (Partiya Karkerên Kurdistanê [The Kurdistan Workers' Party]) for finding peaceful ways to deal with the so-called "Kurdish issue" in Turkey (Volkan, 2013). I was severely accused by some individuals for being someone against Turks or against Kurds.

First, I want to state that people's and large groups' aggressive or libidinal investments are the same anywhere in the world; they may be "normal," or sometimes horribly exaggerated. I give examples of my findings from events which I studied. This does not mean that I chose to humiliate a specific large group. Second, I always approached large-group conflicts by holding on to my psychoanalytic identity. I (or my team members) did not suggest solutions; I only tried to find ways for representatives of large groups to come up with their own ideas for solutions.

Large-group identity

During my decades-long activities in the international arena I have learned that behind observable factors like politics, economics, and legal issues, the central psychological factor in starting and keeping alive large-group conflicts is the protection and maintenance of large-group identity. During my work I heard the subjective experiences of such large-group identities being expressed in terms such as "We are Cypriot Turks," "We are Palestinians," "We are Lithuanian Jews," "We are Russians living in Estonia," "We are Croats," "We are Greek," "We are Communists," "We are Sunni Muslims."

Unlike character and personality, which are observed and perceived by others, identity refers to an individual's inner working model—this person, not an outsider, senses and experiences it. Erik Erikson (1956) defined the subjective experience of *individual identity* that slowly evolves from childhood as a persistent sense of sameness within oneself, while sharing some characteristics with other individuals. Salman Akhtar (1992, 1999) wrote that the sustained feeling of inner sameness is accompanied by a temporal continuity in the self-experience: the past, the present, and the future are integrated into a smooth continuum of remembered, felt, and expected existence for the individual. He also described how individual identity is connected with a realistic body image and a sense of inner solidarity, associated with the capacity for solitude and clarity of one's gender and linked to large-group identity such as a national, ethnic, or religious identity.

Belonging to a large-group identity is part of human existence. Tribal, ethnic, national, religious, and ideological large-group identities exist worldwide. They are the end-result of myths and realities of common beginnings, historical continuities, and geographical realities, and shared cultural, linguistic, religious, and ideological factors. Existing conditions in the environment direct children to invest in this or that type of large-group belongingness. A child born in Hyderabad, India, for example, would focus on religious/cultural issues as she develops a large-group identity, since adults there define their dominant large-group identity according to religious affiliation—Muslim or Hindu (Kakar, 1996). A child born in Cyprus during the hot Cypriot Turk–Cypriot Greek conflict would absorb a dominant large-group identity defined by ethnic/national sentiments, because what was critical in this part of the world at that time was whether one was Greek or Turkish, and less emphasis was placed on whether one was Greek Orthodox Christian or Sunni Muslim (Volkan, 1979a).

Some children have parents who belong to two different ethnic or religious large groups. If an international conflict erupts between these two large groups, these youngsters may, even as adults, suffer psychological problems. In the Republic of Georgia, after the collapse of the Soviet Union, wars between Georgians and South Ossetians especially confused and psychologically disturbed individuals with "mixed" lineage. The same was true in Transylvania for the children born of mixed Romanian and Hungarian marriages, when the hostility between these two large groups was inflamed.

Psychobiological potential for we-ness

Scientific studies of recent decades have shown that the mind of the human infant is remarkably active and there is a psychobiological potential of we-ness and bias toward one's own kind which exists in the early months and years of a child's life (Bloom, 2010; Emde, 1991; Greenspan, 1989; Lehtonen, 2003, Purhonen, Kilpeläinen-Lees, Valkonen-Korhonen, Karhu, & Lehtonen, 2005; Stern, 1985). I must add that this we-ness is limited since an infant's or a small child's experiences are restricted. As time passes, children begin to separate their own mental images from those of familiar others, such as mothers, integrating different aspects, such as pleasant and unpleasant or libidinal and aggressive aspects, of both types of images (Kernberg, 1976; Mahler, 1968; Mahler, Pine, & Bergman, 1975;

Volkan, 1976). At twenty-four to thirty-six months of age, a child's sense of cultural/societal amplifiers—concrete or abstract symbols and signs that are only associated with a particular large group—is present.

Identification

As the child separates and integrates the images of familiar others and his own images he identifies with a range of realistic, fantasied, wished for, or frightening elements of these important individuals. Such identifications also embrace concrete and abstract large-group identity markers such as language, nursery rhymes, and other cultural amplifiers, religious and political beliefs, and historical images. Long ago Sigmund Freud (1940a) noted that parents represent the greater society to their child. This includes identification with the parents' and other important persons' prejudices about Others, ranging from benign to hostile.

Depositing

In "identification" children are the primary actors in collecting images, perceptions, prejudices, and various psychological tasks from their environment and making such things belong to them. Children also become reservoirs of deposited images and evolve various psychological tasks, ranging from maladaptive ones to creative ones, to deal with them. In "depositing" it is an adult in the child's life who feels the need to put unconsciously something into the child's psyche. As a replacement child my self-representation included my grandmother's and mother's images of my dead uncle as well as my important Ottoman namesake and reparative psychological tasks. I have given other examples of depositing in my previous writings (Volkan, 1988, 2013, 2014a; Volkan, Ast, & Greer, 2002).

Psychological DNA

When thousands or millions of children become receivers of the same or a similar deposited image and psychological task, they begin to share the same "psychological DNA." For example, after experiencing a collective catastrophe inflicted by an enemy group, affected individuals are left with self-images similarly (though not identically) traumatized by the massive event. These many individuals deposit such images into their children and give them tasks such as: "Regain my self-esteem for me"; "Put my mourning process on the right track"; "Be assertive and take revenge"; or "Never forget and remain alert." Though each child in the second generation owns an individualized identity, all share similar links to the same massive trauma's image and similar unconscious tasks for coping with it. If the next generation cannot effectively fulfill their shared tasks—and this is usually the case—they will pass them on to the third generation, and so on. Such conditions create a powerful unseen network among thousands or millions of people. Depositing also includes passing along various kinds of prejudicial elements concerning the unfamiliar Other, the stranger.

Shared prejudice

Rene Spitz's (1965) research informed us how infants recognize that not all the faces around them belong to their caregivers. He named his finding as "stranger anxiety" which peaks at from six to twelve months and which is also associated with the initiation of "normal" prejudice. Henry Parens (1979) reminded us that prejudice is not inborn. Parens told us that in the course of normal development, every newborn experiences certain obligatory adaptive reactivities that predispose the child to develop prejudices, whereby the child becomes prejudiced.

My term "suitable targets for externalization" describes how children, at the peak of putting their unmended images together, learn *experientially* about the existence of other large groups and develop shared prejudices (Volkan, 1988).

Suitable targets of externalization

Let us go back to my childhood in Cyprus. Imagine me, at age three, having a picnic next to a Cypriot Greek farm where pigs are wandering about. Also imagine me trying to touch and love a pig. My Muslim grandmother would strongly discourage me from doing so. For Muslim Turks, the pig is "dirty." As a cultural/societal amplifier it does not belong to the Turkish large group, it belongs to Greeks. At age three I still had some unintegrated self-images and internalized object images. Now at the Cypriot Greek farm I found a suitable target for my unwanted, aggressively contaminated, and unintegrated "bad" self- and object images. Since as a Muslim child I did not eat pork, in a concrete sense, what I externalized into the image of the pig would not be re-internalized. Since almost every Turkish child in

Cyprus would use the same target, they would share the same precursor of the unfamiliar Other and invest similar prejudice in this Other.

A Scottish boy slowly becomes aware that a kilt or bagpipe is associated with Scottishness. These items become reservoirs of his unintegrated "good" images. He shares such an experience with all other Scottish boys.

Children use all kinds of cultural/social amplifiers, such as special food, the colors of a flag, churches, mosques, or synagogues, pictures of heroes belonging to their large group or belonging to the Other as suitable targets for externalization for their "good" and "bad" unintegrated images. Sophisticated thoughts, perceptions, and emotions, and knowledge of history about the unfamiliar Other evolve much later without the children's awareness that the experientially learned symbol of the Other was in the service of helping them avoid feeling object relations tension.

Once the child utilizes *shared* suitable targets of externalization, he or she *experientially* starts giving up being a generalist. Now the child has a firmer sense of belonging to a specific large group and separating himself or herself from the shared stranger Other.

We all have prejudices which may have remained benign or due to exposure to various types of life events may become hostile and even malignant. When they have malignant prejudice, individuals kill other human beings. Here I want to emphasize that the concept of "suitable targets for externalization" refers to developing *shared* stranger anxiety and creating *shared* prejudice at the large-group level. Shared prejudices too can stay benign, or can become hostile or malignant.

Second individuation

During an individual's passage through adolescence, there is an unconscious review of childhood attachments to familiar Others. This leads to a youngster's "second individuation." Peter Blos (1962, 1967) described the crystallization of a firm sense of personal and gender identities during the passage through adolescence. I added that during adolescence an individual's large-group identity that has evolved during childhood also becomes a final identity (Volkan, 1997, 2004).

Due to life circumstances during the teen years and adulthood, a person—such as an individual who migrated to another country and settled there during later teen years or early adulthood—may deny or repress her investment in her large-group identity that had evolved during childhood, but this large-group identity stays "alive" in the shadows. As a voluntary immigrant I developed an American identity. However, I am also aware of my Cypriot Turkish identity. Voluntary or forced immigrants have a more comfortable life if they develop a stable biculturalism.

The other

Erik Erikson (1956) theorized that primitive humans sought a measure of protection for their unbearable nakedness by wearing animal skins, feathers, or claws. On the basis of these outer garments, each tribe or clan developed a sense of shared identity, as well as a conviction that it alone harbored the one human identity. He suggested that human beings have evolved into *pseudo species* such as tribes or clans that behave as if they were separate species. Such postulations are supported by references to the Other in many ancient documents and languages. The Apache Indians considered themselves to be *indeh*, the people, and everyone else as *indah*, the enemy (Boyer, 1986). Ancient Chinese regarded themselves as *people* and viewed the Other as *kuei* or "hunting spirits." The Mundurucu in the Brazilian rain forest divided their world into Mundurucu, who were people, and non-Mundurucu, who were *pariwat* (enemies), except for certain neighbors who they perceived as friendly (Murphy, 1957). There are other examples of large groups who consider only themselves as "people," such as the Sudanese Dinka (the name of the group translates as "people") and Nuer ("original people"), and the Arctic Yupiks ("real people") (Harari, 2014).

We can expand Erikson's ideas further. Primitive neighboring groups had to compete for territory, food, sex, and physical goods for their survival. We can imagine that this competition eventually assumed more psychological implications. Physical essentials, besides retaining their status as genuine necessities, absorbed or gave birth to mental meanings as well, such as competition, prestige, honor, power, envy, revenge, humiliation, submission, grief, and mourning. Some of them evolved as large-group cultural/social amplifiers, like a flag or a song, and were linked to historical memories, religions, shared narcissism, and large-group identities.

The psychology of neighbors

For centuries, tribes living in close proximity had only each other to interact with, due to their natural boundaries. In the modern world, large groups develop a neighbor-like psychology without being in close physical proximity. For example, North Korea's missiles and the United States Navy's activities in the Yellow Sea or Sea of Japan, in a psychological sense, make the United States and North Korea neighbors (Suistola & Volkan, 2017; Volkan, 1988, 1997). As I am writing this book the United States and Iran are behaving like two rivals living next door to each other.

Regardless of location on the globe, the psychology of neighbors remains the core issue in a large group's developing an identity for itself as well as an identity for the neighbor and in making enemies and allies.

The need to have enemies and allies

The preoedipal children's externalization of shared libidinal "good" unintegrated images into the same suitable targets of externalization is the beginning of a need to have societal allies. Their externalization of aggressively invested "bad" unintegrated shared images obliges members of a large group to have societal enemies.

Large groups compete like individuals, like children playing in a park. The eternal question is: Which is on the right side: stronger, smarter, more civilized, better looking, simply better? At one end of the spectrum of such competition there is a situation similar to that of the Olympic Games, in which the race is open and benevolent (with the exception of the Games in Munich in 1972 when a group of Palestinian terrorists killed two Israeli athletes and took nine others hostage). At the other end of the spectrum, however, competition may lead to destructive efforts—sometimes secret, other times overt—to ruin the chances of the enemy in an activity in which supremacy is being sought.

Similarity between opposing large groups and the necessity for a psychological gap

When antagonistic large groups are in competition there are two *hidden* principles at work. The first one involves, paradoxically, a perspective of similarity between opposing large groups. Since our enemies, however real they may be, serve as a reservoir of our unwanted selves, they are unconsciously seen to some extent as being like us. On a conscious level, they cannot be the same as us since they contain our unwanted aspects and we vigorously reject those characteristics.

The second principle pertains to what I call a psychological gap between enemy large groups. Although this gap keeps enemies at a distance, it fosters a continuous relationship on both conscious and unconscious levels since each side tries to control it. To this extent there is a common cause in spite of the emphasis on differences. Looking at a daily newspaper of a country in conflict with another will show more preoccupation with the enemy than allies.

The tent metaphor

When I referred to needing enemies and allies, I sounded as if everybody in a large group has identical perceptions and feelings about the Other. In reality many individuals in each country think and feel differently, to one extent or the other, than the persons who have political/military authority. Nevertheless, when there are international conflicts many academics and journalists start talking about countries as if they were single individuals unless a clearly observable political/societal division exists at such times. The tent metaphor demonstrates why we have the tendency to speak of large groups as if they are single individuals.

The classical Freudian theory of large groups can be visualized as people arranged around a gigantic maypole, which represents the group leader. Members of the large group dance around the pole/leader, identifying with each other and idealizing the leader and attempting to identify with the leader. I have expanded this maypole metaphor by imagining a canvas extending from the pole out over all the people, forming a huge tent (Volkan, 1992).

Now let us think in terms of how we learn to wear two layers, like fabric, from the time we are children. The first layer, the individual layer, fits each of us snugly, like clothing. It is one's core personal identity that provides an inner sense of persistent sameness for the individual. From an individual psychology point of view, the second layer, the canvas of the tent, may be perceived as a breast–mother and the pole can be a symbol of an oedipal father. From a large-group psychology point of view the canvas of the tent represents the large-group identity that is shared by thousands or millions of people, including the political leader, the pole, whose primary task is to hold the tent erect and protect and maintain large-group identity.

Each tent is surrounded by neighboring tents but the designs stitched on the canvas of one large-group's tent are different to those stitched on the others. Instead of focusing on thousands or millions of people under a tent who individually may have some disagreements, we usually refer to the name of the tent, such as Catalan or Japanese or Muslim, while describing relationships between large groups.

Suitable targets of externalization
during large-group conflicts

When stressed, as in times of war or war-like situations, adults under a large-group tent revert to their original childish ways of binding with one another and seek abstract or concrete items as suitable targets of externalization. They may actually search for inanimate or nonhuman objects as highly significant tokens. I will give two examples:

> When the Cypriot Turks were living in enclaves in subhuman conditions surrounded by Cypriot Greeks, they turned to a shared hobby of raising parakeets (parakeets are not native birds in Cyprus). There were thousands of these parakeets in cages everywhere, in people's homes or in grocery stores. They represented the Cypriot Turks' imprisoned and needy selves. The large group took care of the caged birds, and in turn unconsciously maintained an illusion that they themselves were being cared for. This is how they were able to survive psychologically through eleven very difficult years. (Volkan, 1979a)

In 1981 I was attending, as a facilitator, the American Psychiatric Association's committee-sponsored meeting between Israelis and Egyptians in Switzerland. For the first time Palestinians were also present. In a small group gathering, an intelligent and mature Palestinian sat next to an Israeli general who used to be in charge of the occupied territories. Sitting next to an important Israeli in a neutral country as an equal was rather difficult for him, and he seemed to regress. At one point, he became very emotional and told us that we could do many things to him, but we could not rob him of his source of spiritual power. He went on to say that as long as he had a certain inanimate object in his pocket he could be threatened with death but he would not give up his Palestinian identity (Volkan, 2013). After this event I studied the existence of these highly significant inanimate tokens in the Gaza Strip at that time. Almost all Palestinians knew of their existence and they made use of them. They were made of small pieces of stone, painted with Palestinian national colors. These stones provided a shared reservoir of ethnicity and nationality.

Shared jokes

After a massive trauma, usually shared jokes circulate. Following the devastating earthquake in Mexico in 1985 when an estimated 10,000 died and when serious damage occurred in the nation's capital, people in Mexico would ask: "What is the similarity between a doughnut [a pastry with a circle shape with a space in the middle] and Mexico City?" The answer was that the middle of both a doughnut and Mexico City was missing. If people make jokes about their own losses it is an indication that in the long run the members of a large group will get over the shared trauma. Laughter is a reversal of sad affects that helps the survivors to discharge their emotions, confirm their remaining alive, and deal with their survival guilt through denial.

Jokes following a disaster at the hand of the Other are different. People do not make fun of their own dead and things they lost. In their jokes there is direct reference to the "badness" of the enemy. For example, when I studied Kuwaiti society after the invasion of this country by Saddam Hussein's forces, I noted that most jokes referred to Iraqi soldiers not knowing the difference between eatable animals, such as a lamb, and uneatable animals in a zoo, such as a tiger. The invaders were presented as stupid individuals. On the surface, degrading the enemy increases the victimized large group's shared narcissism. A closer look indicates shame and degeneration within the victimized people. Apparently, the invading Iraqi soldiers had opened the doors of animal cages in the zoo in Kuwait City. They raped Kuwaiti women and locked up one or two of them naked in these emptied cages. Whether this story was true or not did not matter. What mattered was the Kuwaitis' belief that such degrading events took place. Laughter after the zoo jokes deep down expressed an attempted denial or reversal of humiliation of large-group identity. Kuwaiti young men generalized the idea of raped women incidents and thus for some time they wanted to postpone marriage with the (unconscious) idea that the women they would marry were also those who had been raped. The nature of initial jokes after a massive trauma can give some indications about how the large group will recover in the long run.

Transgenerational transmissions

During World War II Anna Freud and Dorothy Burlingham (1942), and later other psychoanalysts such as Margaret Mahler (1968), described how there is fluidity between a mother's (mothering person's) and child's psychic borders, and the mother's anxiety, unconscious fantasies, perceptions, and expectations of the external world, including those relating to her child, can pass into the child's developing sense of self. It is also known that psychic borders can be permeable in a relationship between a grown child and parent, or between two adult individuals when they relate to one another under drastically regressed or even partly regressed states.

After living in surrounded enclaves filled with garbage in horrible conditions for eleven years Cypriot Turks found freedom in 1974. However, they continued to keep their environment dirty by throwing empty bottles and food packages on neighbors' gardens or on highways while driving from one place to another. Four years ago, I was appointed as the honorary chairperson of a North Cyprus presidential committee called "Think Clean." I concluded that the difficulty to keep the environment clean in North Cyprus had a connection to the population's transmitted "memory" of living in enclaves in extremely dirty surroundings. I shared my observation with the committee members. This situation in North Cyprus is slowly getting better.

The most significant way transgenerational transmission occurs is through depositing. Anne Ancelin Schützenberger's "ancestor syndrome" (1998), Judith Kestenberg's term "transgenerational transposition" (1982), Haydée Faimberg's description of "the telescoping of generations" (2005), and many other psychoanalysts' works on the intergenerational transmissions of Holocaust related images and ego functions (for example see: Brenner, 2014, 2019; Kogan, 1995; Laub & Podell, 1997; Volkan, Ast, & Greer, 2002) refer to depositing.

Passing traumatized images and psychological tasks to the next generation is closely related to the traumatized individual's difficulty in mourning. If losses are accompanied by traumatic events, mourning becomes complicated, because the mourner has to deal with accompanying feelings, such as helplessness, humiliation, and rage, as well as aggressive, vengeful, or masochistic thoughts. This creates a troublesome psychological condition, whereby the mourner unconsciously may assign the task of mourning to his or her offspring along with the images linked to the original trauma and other tasks dealing with these images. Similar processes may also appear in the victimizer's descendants. Among the perpetrators' descendants there is more preoccupation with consequences of shared feelings of guilt than preoccupation with shared feelings of helplessness. Both large groups share a severe difficulty: the inability to mourn.

Mourning

Mourning occurs because the human mind does not allow the reality of a significant loss to be accepted without an internal struggle. When I speak of mourning, I am not referring to the "acute grief" of people in shock and/or in pain, who may experience crying spells, frustration, anger, numbness, and withdrawal from their environment. The physical burial of a corpse, or the disappearance of a family home by fire, does not remove the mental images of these lost entities from the mourner's mind. The mourner continues to have an internal relationship with these images. Mourning is a slow process of internally reviewing our real as well as wished-for or even feared relationship with the lost person or thing again and again until the reality of the loss or change is emotionally accepted (Freud, 1917e).

"Normal" individual mourning comes to a practical end after a year or so (if there is no complication) when the images of the lost person or thing no longer preoccupy the mourner's mind with full force. The mental representation (collection of images) of the deceased (or the lost thing) becomes "futureless" (Tähkä, 1984). For example, a woman stops fantasizing that a husband who had been dead for some time will give her sexual pleasure. Or, a man stops wishing to boss his underlings at a job from which he had been fired years before. The mental images of the lost object may be temporarily activated during some special occasions such as the anniversary of the loss.

One outcome of mourning is a "healthy" and selective identification with the mental images of what was lost. This leads to an enrichment of the mourner's self-representation, since the tasks that once were performed for the mourner by the lost person or thing can now be mastered and performed by the mourner himself.

A very different outcome occurs when the mourner identifies "in toto" (Ritvo & Solnit, 1958, p. 70) with the representation of what was lost. This non-selective identification causes problems because the mourner identifies with both the loved and hated aspects or functions of the lost person or thing. What used to be ambivalence and struggle with the representation of what was lost now becomes ambivalence toward the mourner's own self and initiates an internal struggle. The mourner feels depressed (Freud, 1917e). When the loss is accompanied by traumatic events, humiliation, and helplessness the mourner may become a perennial mourner.

Perennial mourning, linking objects, and linking phenomena

Most individuals with perennial mourning utilize certain inanimate objects such as a special photograph (and also, but seldom, an animate object such as a pet) that symbolize a meeting ground between the object representation of a lost person or thing and the mourner's corresponding self-representation. I call such objects *linking objects* (Volkan, 1981; Volkan &

Zintl, 1993). Mourners "choose" a linking object from various items available in their environment. A linking object may be a personal possession of the deceased, often something the deceased wore or used routinely, like a watch. A gift the deceased made to the mourner before death or a letter written by a soldier on a battlefield before being killed may evolve into a linking object. Then there are what I call "last minute objects," something at hand when a mourner first learned of the death or saw the dead body. They relate to the last moment in which the deceased was regarded as a living person.

Once an item truly evolves as a linking object, the perennial mourner experiences it as "magical." The mourner may hide it, but needs to know the linking object's whereabouts; it must be protected and controlled. Since a person can control an inanimate thing more easily than an animate thing, most linking objects are inanimate items. If a linking object is lost, the perennial mourner will experience anxiety, often severe.

Through the creation of a linking object or phenomenon, the perennial mourner makes an "adjustment" to the complication within the mourning process; the mourner makes the mourning process "unending" so as not to face the conflict pertaining to the relationship with the object repre- sentation of the deceased. By controlling the linking object, perennial mourners control their wish to "bring back" (love) or "kill" (hate) the lost person, thus avoiding the psychological consequences if any of these two wishes are gratified. If the dead person comes back to life, the mourner will depend on him or her forever. The gratification of this wish would have a negative consequence. If the dead person is "killed," the mourner's existing anger will cause feelings of guilt. The gratification of this wish too would have an unwelcome ending.

More importantly, since the linking object or phenomenon is "out there," the mourner's mourning process too is *externalized*. The linking object in the external world contains the tension between ambivalence and anger pertaining to the narcissistic hurt inflicted on the mourner by the death or another type of loss. When mourners "lock up" a photograph that has become a linking object in a drawer, they also "hide" their complicated mourning process in the same drawer. Such people may unlock the drawer during an anniversary of the loss and look at the photograph or touch it. But as soon as they feel anxious, the photograph is locked up again.

When I first wrote about linking objects and linking phenomena, I referred to the clinical cases where they appeared. Thus, I focused on their pathological use. I thought that having linking objects or phenomena always prevents the individual from completing his or her mourning process. Later, in some cases, I began noting their relation to creativity and their use as stepping-stones to adaptive solutions in the mourning process (Volkan, 1999b). The story of a man who, as a child, lost his father during World War II is an illustration of the adaptive use of a linking object. During the war his father used to send home cartoon drawings from the battlefront. The son used these drawings as linking objects in his childhood and teen years. As an adult, he re-internalized the meaning of the linking objects, in other words, he was able to identify with his father's image. Like his father, he used his pen creatively and became a graphic designer.

Linking objects and phenomena should not be confused with childhood transitional objects and phenomena that are reactivated in adulthood. Certainly there are some severely regressed adults, such as some with psychosis, who reactivate the transitional relatedness of their babyhoods and "recreate" transitional objects. A transitional object represents the first not-me, but it is never totally not-me. It links not-me with mother-me and it is a temporary construction toward a sense of reality (Greenacre, 1969; Winnicott, 1953). Linking objects contain high-level symbolism. They must be thought of as tightly packed symbols whose significance is bound up in the conscious and unconscious nuances of the relationship that preceded the loss. Therefore, not every keepsake or memento cherished by a mourner should be considered as a linking object possessing a significant investment of symbolism and magic.

Large-group mourning

A large-group mourning does not refer to all or many members crying openly or talking about their losses. Large-group mourning manifests itself by different means. One of them is to modify some existing societal processes or initiate new ones. For example, following the deaths of 116 children and 28 adults in an avalanche of coal slurry in the Welsh village of Aberfan on October 21, 1966, there was a significant increase in the birth rate among women in the village, who had not themselves lost a child, within the five years following the tragedy (Williams & Parkes, 1975). The Aberfan tragedy was not caused deliberately by Others; it was an "act of God." Therefore, there was no humiliation as a result of the tragedy, and the society found a way to balance their losses with gains: more new babies than the statistical average.

In the 1930s, the Jewish population in Warsaw, Poland was about 30 percent of the city's population. The incredible tragedy they went through at the hands of the Nazis is well known. When I visited Warsaw in 2019, I was emotionally reminded what had happened to Jews at this location. I also realized the psychological significance of another event when a well-educated tourist guide took me to the Old Town and spoke how during the Warsaw Uprising in August 1944, more than 85 percent of this historic center was destroyed by Nazi troops. But, a five-year reconstruction campaign by Warsaw's citizens resulted in meticulous restoration of the Old Town. Listening to the tour guide I realized that this physical restoration also stood for a psychological restoration, the restoration of the citizens' self-esteem and providing them with a sense of pride.

I wrote about what happened in Aberfan and Warsaw in order to illustrate how communities, and also large groups, sometimes find adaptive ways of dealing with losses.

When there are severe complications in large-group mourning, transmissions of images of historical events shared by members of a large group and psychological tasks linked to them may lead to the development of chosen traumas and chosen glories.

Chosen traumas and chosen glories

The most significant designs attached to the canvas of the metaphorical tent that play key roles in the large group's interactions with another large group are "chosen traumas" and "chosen glories." A chosen trauma is the shared mental image of a historical event within a large group where the group's ancestors suffered catastrophic loss, humiliation, and helplessness at the hands of their enemies, where there is an inability to mourn those losses. The word "chosen" is not to imply that a large group "chooses" to be victimized by another large group and subsequently loses self-esteem. It does, however, recognize that the group "chooses" to psychologize and dwell on a past traumatic event and make it a major large-group identity marker on the metaphorical large-group tent's canvas. Czechs commemorate the battle of Bila Hora in 1620, which led to their subjugation under the Hapsburg Empire for nearly 300 years; Scots keep alive the story of the battle of Culloden in 1746 and the failure of Bonnie Prince Charlie to restore a Stuart to the British throne; the Dakota Indians of the United States recall the anniversary of their decimation at Wounded Knee in 1890.

Not every shared historical trauma becomes a chosen trauma. The mental representation of the Battle of Kosovo which took place in 1389 between the Ottomans and the Serbs became the Serbians' chosen trauma due to following developments. The myth developed among the Serbs some seventy years after the Battle of Kosovo, whereby the event and the Serbian characters of this battle—especially the Serbian leader Prince Lazar who was killed—mingled with elements and characters of Christianity. As decades passed, Prince Lazar became associated with Jesus Christ, and icons showing Lazar's representation in fact decorated many Serbian churches throughout the six centuries following the battle. Throughout generations songs and poems reminded the people of the Battle of Kosovo. Even during the communist period when the government discouraged hero worship, Serbs were able to drink (introject) a popular red wine called "Prince Lazar" (Sells, 2002; Volkan, 1996, 1997).

Chosen glories are shared mental images of pride and pleasure-evoking ancestral events and heroes that are recollected ritualistically. For example, each November, Americans ritualistically celebrate Thanksgiving, a national holiday that commemorates a feast held by the European immigrants (Pilgrims) of the Plymouth settlement in Massachusetts after their first successful harvest in 1621. Today, Thanksgiving is a celebration in which special foods, such as turkey and pumpkin pie, are eaten and expressions of gratitude are given for a wide range of things that Americans have to be thankful for. There is considerable evidence to suggest that many of the notions that Americans believe to be historical facts about the first years of Pilgrim life in North America have been significantly altered or replaced by myths over the centuries (Furman, 1998). Thanksgiving thus represents a type of chosen glory that idealizes the "birth" of the American nation, marking American togetherness and large-group identity.

There is another chosen glory in the United States that, unlike Thanksgiving, when utilized causes a severe societal division. Let us recall how events in Charlottesville motivated me to write this book. White nationalist groups in the United States perceive white superiority, identification with the Third Reich, holding on to anti-Semitism as a lost chosen glory and wish to recapture it.

Sometimes chosen traumas and chosen glories appear as intertwined. I described these concepts for the first time in 1991 after I noticed how representatives of opposing large groups in a dialogue series would suddenly refer to such events when they sense that their opponents belittled the first large group's image (Volkan, 1991a).

Here is an example: After the collapse of the Soviet Union, Estonians gained their independence. However, every third person in Estonia at that time was not an Estonian. He or she was a Russian or a "Russian speaker"—a non-Estonian person who had belonged to the former Soviet Union. Overnight the Estonians had become the administrators of their own country, while Russians and Russian speakers—most of them now noncitizens—were left in a state of great confusion. There was also a border dispute between Estonia and Russia. My facilitating team from the Center for the Study of Mind and Human Interaction (CSMHI) brought together influential Estonians and Russians, such as parliamentarians and well-known academics and public figures, for three days of unofficial diplomatic discussions. We had two meetings in 1994, seven meetings in 1995, and another two meetings in 1996. The Estonians' chosen trauma is unrelated to one specific historical event, but to the fact that they had lived under almost constant dominance of the Other (Danes, Poles, Swedes, Germans, Russians) for many centuries. After gaining independence, Estonians were singing and celebrating their newly found freedom. However, my team members and I could see how, psychologically speaking, they had become anxious with their unconscious expectation for disappearing as an independent country once more. During the initial part of the dialogue series we could see anger on some Estonian team members' faces, but they would not verbalize their negative feelings against their most recent occupiers. Toward the end of the second year of the dialogue series the Estonian participants started to be more comfortable in referring to their victimization under the Soviet regime, expressing their negative feelings towards Russians to their Russian counterparts.

During one session we were discussing some current issues when an Estonian complained about the Russians' past treatment of his people. A very high-level person from the Russian parliament, who was a member of the Russian dialogue team, suddenly and very loudly began talking about events that took place from the thirteenth to the fifteenth century: Tatar and Mongol lords occupying many parts of today's Russia, including Moscow. I recall how my facilitating team members and I were surprised. The Russian parliamentarian could not stop talking about what has become known to historians as "the Tatar–Mongol yoke" (see for example, Halperin, 2009). The Russian chosen trauma had come alive in the room.

The parliamentarian wanted us to realize that the victimized Russians had stood between the Tatar and Mongol perpetrators and the Europeans.

If Russia had not existed, the Europeans would have been devastated by the Tatars and Mongols. He was upset that the Europeans did not acknowledge how Russian suffering had saved the Europeans. He described the Russians' entitlement to rule over other large groups, but at the same time being different than the Tatars and Mongols through a behavior that protected the Others under the Russian rule. How dare the Estonians not appreciate living under Russian rule which had brought "good" things to Estonia! I noted that the parliamentarian not only was talking about the Russian chosen trauma but he also was glorifying victimized ancestors who, he believed, had protected the Europeans from a disaster.

In 2006 I was a visiting scholar at the University of Vienna's Political Science Department in Austria. I had eighty students from different countries. To illustrate people's emotional investment in their large-group identities that develops in childhood—even when these persons in their routine daily lives are not thinking about such investment—and observe how ancestral history induces intense feelings as if such events had taken place yesterday, I designed an experiment. I chose five students from Poland and five students from Turkey. I asked them to study in depth the history of the Ottoman Turks' two-month siege of Vienna, followed by their defeat by forces under the Polish King John III Sobieski on September 12, 1683. A week later these ten students presented what they had studied in front of the whole class and some visitors. It became clearly observable how the Polish and Turkish students—like the unofficial representatives of opposing national or ethnic groups my team and I had brought together—had become spokespersons of their nationalistic large-group identities, and how they were exhibiting the nature of these identities with strong emotions. It was as if the Ottomans' siege of Vienna was reoccurring. A few years later, when I was a guest professor at Bahçeşehir University in Istanbul, Turkey, I chose other Polish and Turkish students and repeated this experiment—eliciting the same result.

A chosen trauma is not an image of a rather recent historical event. For example, the Holocaust that links all Jewish persons together, whether they were directly affected by Nazis or not, is not a chosen trauma. Survivors' pictures and some belongings are still at the descendants' homes, and survivors' stories are still "alive." Over many generations an individual, his or her parents, grandparents, other relatives, and friends will have no actual memory of the ancestors' trauma. The mental image of the ancestors' trauma undergoes a process which was named by Robert Waelder (1936) as change of function. Now it is perceived as a significant symbol that psychologically links the large-group members together.

Usually no complicated psychological processes are involved when chosen glories are reactivated unless the chosen glory is a shared fantasy like the one white supremacist groups in the United States possess. The reactivation of chosen traumas, in supporting large-group identity and its cohesiveness, is more complex. Chosen traumas are stronger large-group amplifiers because of their link to ancestors' complicated mourning. When a chosen trauma (or a fantasied chosen glory like the one white supremacist groups share) is reactivated the entitlement ideology which is linked to it also becomes inflamed.

Entitlement ideology

The term "entitlement ideology" refers to a large group's members feeling entitled to regain what their ancestors lost centuries ago, a narcissistic reorganization accompanied by hostile prejudice for the descendants of the ancestor's enemy or, through shared displacement, a current enemy (Volkan, 1996, 2018a). An entitlement ideology remains dormant for some time, but political leaders and malignant propaganda can easily inflame it. The Serbian entitlement ideology is known as Christoslavism (Sells, 2002). The fall of Constantinople (today's Istanbul), the capital of the Byzantine Empire, in 1453 is the Greeks' chosen trauma and it is linked to Greeks' entitlement ideology which is called the *Megali Idea* (Great Idea) (Volkan & Itzkowitz, 1994).

The Megali Idea has played a role in the initiation and maintenance of ethnic troubles in Cyprus. Well-known sociologist Kyriacos Markides (1977) who was born in Cyprus stated:

> Because the Greeks of Cyprus have considered themselves historically and culturally to be Greeks, the "Great Idea" has had an intense appeal. Thus, when the church fathers called on the Cypriots [Cypriot Greeks] to fight for union with Greece, it did not require much effort to heat up emotions … Enosis [uniting Cyprus with Greece] did not originate in the church but in the minds of intellectuals in their attempt to revive Greek-Byzantine civilization. (Markides, 1977, p. 10)

Time collapse

While conducting unofficial diplomatic dialogues my team members and I did not deal with any one individual's psychological issues. These gatherings were not intended to be therapeutic for anyone. We listened to participants from opposing parties as representatives of their large groups and focused on large-group psychology. When these individuals became preoccupied with chosen traumas and chosen glories, we became aware of a situation which I named as "time collapse" (Volkan, 1997, 1999a). It refers to magnifying the image of the current enemies and current conflicts after the reactivation of shared feelings, fantasies, expectations, and defenses associated with chosen trauma or chosen glory, especially the former one. During unofficial diplomatic dialogues and also during official ones the time collapse leads to obstacles against participants' exploring peaceful solutions. Generally speaking, during official diplomatic negotiations facilitators do not pay attention to or even realize the existence of such psychological resistances.

Time collapse due to manipulation of politicians or other influential persons within large groups, may lead to "dehumanization."

Dehumanization

If a conflict between two large groups intensifies and continues, one large group may begin to perceive the other as less human, so that it becomes more suitable for absorbing shared externalizations and projections. First, the other group is seen as human but bad; later they become dehumanized (Bernard, Ottenberg, & Redl, 1973; Moses,1990).

In the spring of 1990, I had an opportunity to study a Palestinian orphanage, Beit Atfal al-Sumud (the House of Steadfast Children), in Tunis. Beit Atfal al-Sumud was first opened in Lebanon in 1976 to provide a place for orphaned Palestinian children from the destroyed Tel al-Za'atar district. On September 15, 1982, Israeli defense forces encircled two adjacent Palestinian refugee camps, Sabra and Shatila, in West Beirut. In the late afternoon of the following day, the Lebanese Christian Phalangist militia, allies of the Israelis, attacked the camps, indiscriminately killing civilians trapped in the cramped streets. Because of this tragedy, another 1,300 Palestinian children needed looking after. Beit Atfal al-Sumud had a branch in Tunis. When I visited this place, it housed thirty-one boys and twenty-one girls ranging from age seven to eighteen, and five children who had been rescued as infants from the massacres at Sabra and Shatila (Volkan, 2014b). My focus here is not their histories, but on their dehumanizing the Israelis.

Many of them had heard about a Jewish shopkeeper in Tunis and had gone to see him. They were very surprised to meet a very kind, old man with a smiling face. In their minds this did not match their fixed ideas about Jewish people. Eventually they agreed that maybe the Jewish shopkeeper in Tunis was alright, but the Israelis as a whole were bad. When I inquired whether they had ever seen an Israeli face-to-face, they told me that they had seen Israelis on television. "They look like humans, but they are not human," they kept repeating.

Demonizing and dehumanizing Others by the Nazis is well known. In Rwanda, in 1994, the Hutu first referred to the Tutsi as evil, and later began calling them *cafards*. Meaning cockroaches. Then a mass slaughter of Tutsi and moderate Hutu, a malignant purification, took place between April 7 and July 15.

Purification

Like a snake shedding its skin, a large group will cast off certain elements such as symbols or ideologies that no longer seem appropriate, or those things that seem to impede the revitalization of large-group identity and sometimes threatening Others (Volkan, 1997, 1999a, 1999c, 1999d, 2004).

Here are historical examples of benign purification: During the almost 400-year Ottoman rule of Greek-speaking territories, Turkish words entered the Greek language creating a "hybrid" that was both familiar and different to those who spoke Greek or Turkish. Many Greeks became Turcophone, speaking Turkish but writing in Greek letters. After the Greeks won their independence from the Ottoman Empire (1821–1833) they slowly consolidated a new Greek identity based on elements of Hellenism and the heritage of the Byzantine Empire (Herzfeld,1986; Volkan & Itzkowitz, 1994), they created *Katharevusa*, a neo-classical form of the Greek language. After Latvia gained its independence from the Soviet Union, its people wanted to get rid of some twenty Russian bodies in their national cemetery. In today's Ukraine the population is strongly encouraged to speak Ukrainian not Russian.

Following September 11, 2001, we noticed tendencies of hostile purification in the United States. In one case, a man was killed because, to the killer's mind, he looked Arabic. The best example of malignant purification that I studied had occurred in Serbia under the leadership of Slobodan Milošević. He and people around him inflamed the Serbian chosen trauma, the shared mental representation of the Battle of Kosovo which I mentioned above. This led to time collapse, dehumanization, and purification with terrible, deadly consequences against Muslim Bosnians and Kosovar Albanians (Volkan, 1997). Bad as this process was, the genocide that occurred during the Nazi period still stands as the most horrible example of malignant purification.

Understanding the meaning and psychological necessity of purifications can help to develop strategies to keep shared prejudices within "normal" limits and from becoming malignant and destructive.

Minor differences and the maintenance of non-sameness

During my youth when I travelled in Cyprus in a car, I would see shepherds looking after their animals. From a distance I could tell who was a Greek Cypriot shepherd and who was a Turkish Cypriot one. Between them there was a minor difference. The Greek shepherd would tie a blue cloth around his belt and the Turkish a red one. The inhabitants of Andhra Pradesh in India often wear scarves around their necks, whereas members of the neighboring group, the Telanganas, do not.

The term "minor differences" was coined by Sigmund Freud (1918a) (also see: Freud, 1917e, 1921c, 1930a). Freud initially described such differences between the individuals but then also wrote about this concept as it appeared between large groups. He wrote:

> It is always possible to bind together a considerable number of people in love, so long as there are other people left over to receive the manifestation of their aggressiveness ... it is precisely communities with adjoining territories, and related to each other in other ways as well, who are engaged in constant feuds and in ridiculing each other—like the Spaniards and the Portuguese, for instance, the North Germans and the South Germans, the English and Scotch, and so on. I gave this phenomenon the name of "narcissism of minor differences," a name which does not do much to explain it. We can now see that it is a convenient and relatively harmless satisfaction of the inclination to aggression, by means of

which cohesion between the members of the community is made easier. (1930a, p. 114)

David Werman (1988) reviewed Freud's ideas about this term and stated that "In contrast to Freud's observation that the narcissism of minor differences is relatively harmless, I suggest that in the social sphere it harbors the potential for a pernicious escalation into hostile and destructive actions on a widespread scale" (p. 451).

When large groups are in conflict, any signal of similarity is perceived, often unconsciously, as unacceptable; minor differences therefore become elevated to great importance to protect non-sameness. In times of stress and violent outbreaks, identifying minor differences may have deadly implications. Sinhalese mobs in the Sri Lankan riots of 1958, for example, relied on a variety of subtle indicators—such as the presence of earring holes in the ear or the manner in which a shirt was worn—to identify their enemy Tamils, whom they then attacked or killed (Horowitz, 1985). Between Croats and Serbs, dialect differences—such as the Croat *mlijeko* (milk) vs. the Serb *mleko*—sometimes carry a heavy political–cultural load.

Minor differences become major ones in order to maintain the distinctions between the two large groups and the psychological border between them.

Border psychology

Large-group psychology in its own right also informs us about "psychological borders." When there is no extensive conflict between neighboring large groups, a physical border remains simply a physical border; when there is a conflict, the physical border assumes great psychological meaning as the border separating large-group identities. A physical border becomes a psychological border when unconsciously it is perceived as the canvas of the large-group tent by the majority of members of that large group.

During the Cold War, the Berlin Wall stood as the ultimate symbol of the physical as well as psychological border between the East and the West. Donald Winnicott (1969) reminded us that, while this man-made barricade was unsightly and was completely disassociated from "beauty," without the Berlin Wall, there would have been a war in the 1960s. Winnicott went on to further elucidate the beneficial aspect of the Wall.

He argued that a dividing line between opposing forces, at its worst postpones conflict and at its best holds opposing forces away from each other for long periods of time so that people may play and pursue the arts of peace. The arts of peace belong to the temporary success of a dividing line between opposing forces, the lull between times when the wall has ceased to segregate good and bad.

A few months after the reunification of Germany, I visited a psychoanalyst friend who lived in a town on the west side of the former East German/West German border. He asked if I would like to see the former border and then drove us to a grassy area not far from Göttingen that, prior to 1990, had been on the boundary between the two German states. My friend described how the trees had been cut down to aid the border guards in apprehending defectors. That day, of course, there were no soldiers, and the watchtowers were empty. I was, however, struck by the eerie silence of the place, and also by the way my friend was whispering. It was as though there was still danger in this former border region. We then drove across the old border and into former East Germany, something my friend had not done since before Germany's division. Though they had been reunited, the physical disparities between the two former countries were immediately obvious: the roads were poorly maintained and designed and even the shape of the electric poles was different. It was indisputable that we were now in a different "country."

As we rode through the countryside my friend took a deep breath and then asked me if I smelled something foul. I could not detect anything out of the ordinary, and told him so, but he did not accept my answer. He pointed to a car that was quite a distance in front of us and said: "You see that car? It's communist-made. Those cars smell." I was certain he could not have realistically sensed anything emanating from the car because it was too far away. It seemed that since he "knew" communist-made cars had an offensive odor, his senses played a trick on him. Seeing the car stimulated his smelling the car. My friend was externalizing and projecting some unacceptable elements of his own onto East Germans. He was "clean;" East Germans "stunk." I did not verbalize my deduction but sensed that my friend had come to a similar conclusion about his experience. He seemed embarrassed and quickly changed the topic of conversation.

After this incident at the University of Virginia's Center for the Study of Mind and Human Interaction (CSMHI) a group of academics from different backgrounds studied the border psychology initiated by the German reunification (Volkan, 1997, 1999c). We also noted other investigators' findings. For example, Dieter Ohlmeier (1991) noted that the reunification of Germany was not only a major political change, but was also a major psychological event, prompting a new wave of renegotiations with the Nazi past. Among these renegotiations within German society was the "Nazi skinhead" movement, a maladaptive manifestation of shame and guilt derivations related to the mental representation of the Third Reich (Rosenthal, 1997; Streeck-Fischer ,1999). As Ohlmeier (1991) suggested, psychoanalytic considerations of the German reunification evoked questions of psychology for Germans, and the necessity of a psychohistorical reflection of the Germans since 1933. The studies by CSMHI and others also have shown that certain images related to the Third Reich and the Holocaust (that individuals did not wish to own) and their associated affects and fantasies had been externalized, projected, and displaced from one side of the border to the other. The destabilization of the "location" of these images, fantasies, and affects played a role in the attempts at a fresh method for self-examination of the Nazi past and at a "new" German identity. It took many years after the reunification for the "new" German identity to become solidified by all Germans.

Here is a summary of my observations of another physical border between two antagonistic large groups and how it also became a psychological border. In 1986, when tensions between Israelis and Jordanians were high, as a guest of the Israelis, I visited the Allenby Bridge over the Jordan River that separates the two countries. A white line drawn in the middle of the bridge divided the two countries. At that time, sixteen particular trucks were allowed to pass through the border. Trucks that went over the bridge looked like the factory had forgotten to finish them: doors and hoods were missing, and even the upholstery had been removed to allow no places to hide contraband items. In spite of this, Israeli customs officers would spend hours taking vehicles apart and putting them back together to ensure that nothing was smuggled in from Jordan. At a "jewelry shop" located at the customs building, gold rings and bracelets of every Arab woman were evaluated as they came in and went out of Israel in order to ensure that these women left nothing valuable for their Arab relatives living in Israel. The idea was that if gold was left for Israeli Arabs, they might buy "dangerous" things to be used against Israeli Jews. In another precaution, the Israelis routinely swept a dirt road that ran parallel to the border in order to detect the footprints of people trying to cross it. It should be noted that the border was amply supplied with sophisticated electronic surveillance devices; an Israeli officer informed me, perhaps jokingly, that through electronic surveillance the Israeli authorities could even know when an important person in Jordan went to the bathroom or when he visited a woman who was not his wife. Even if there was justification for the extra precaution, the idea of a psychological border was intertwined with the physical border at the Allenby Bridge, resulting in rituals that created a psychological gap between the two countries.

Large-group regression and progression

I borrow the word "regression" from individual psychology since I have not yet found a good term that describes a large group's "going back" to primitive levels of psychological functioning. Earlier I stated how Robert Waelder (1936) reminded us that Sigmund Freud's (1921c) group psychology, rallying around a leader and large group members' identifying with one another, focuses on regressed groups.

Otto Kernberg (2003a, 2003b) and other psychoanalysts wrote how large groups become involved in paranoid and narcissistic reorganization when they regress and utilize primitive defense mechanisms such as projection, introjection, splitting, avoidance, and denial.

The best example of paranoid organization I observed came from Albania when I visited this country twice and examined the large group processes after the death of dictator Enver Hoxha (Volkan, 2004). Under the totalitarian regime of Enver Hoxha Albanians built 7,500 bunkers throughout their country in anticipation of an enemy attack that never occurred. Building these bunkers, which would not stand against modern weapons, was a reflection of magical thinking and paranoid organization. At the present time, we see various types of magical thinking, such as the expansion of religious fundamentalism at many locations of the world and the increased belief in "whitism" in the USA.

I do not mind calling an event such as the population's "eating up" political propaganda without making much of an effort to evaluate its validity as "shared introjections." An example of "shared introjection" was provided by Michael Šebek (1996) after the collapse of the Soviet Union. In totalitarian regimes, people rally around the leader in order to feel personally secure rather than to be punished by the authorities for disobeying the "rules" of the regime. Michael Šebek described how the population under such regimes introjected "totalitarian objects," and blindly followed their leader by giving up many aspects of their individuality.

Now I want to give an example of splitting in a large group. The existence of an authoritarian government in Turkey is well known. For nearly two decades the leadership of this government, alongside many positive accomplishments, has been trying to change the large-group identity of the Turkish Republic, which was founded in 1923 under the leadership of Kemal Atatürk following the collapse of the Ottoman Empire, to make the country more religious and to erode Turkey's secular traditions. When I was attending the medical school in Ankara in the early 1950s almost half of my classmates were women. None of them covered their faces. During recent years when I went to Turkey to give lectures, I saw women sitting in front of me, half of them showing their faces freely and the other half wearing headscarves as if each group had come from a different ethnic and cultural background.

Shared primitive mechanisms in regressed large groups should be considered only when many members of a large group are dealing with interactions linked to large-group identity issues and when they relate to the Other who has a different large-group identity. Primitive mechanisms, such as projection and splitting, are not utilized during these individuals' routine daily activities while they are relating to family members, friends, or people at a workplace. To think the opposite would only create an absurd illusion in which when a large group is regressed the individuals exhibit borderline or other primitive personality organizations. When societal splitting occurs within the same large group, individuals from both sides go through their daily lives without using patho-logical projection or splitting mechanisms in routine activities.

We must be careful when applying concepts from individual psychology to large-group psychology in its own right. Since large groups as I have described them have their own specific characteristics that are built upon their centuries-old continua and shared mental images of history and myth, the examination of signs and symptoms of their regression should include shared psychodynamics that are specific to each group at a specific time. We need therefore to go beyond a general description of the emergence of shared paranoid or narcissistic sentiments, and refer to specific societal/political manifestations of regression within each large group, such as the inflammation of a chosen trauma, initiating time collapse, and being involved in dehumanization and purification. It is important to describe large-group regression by examining the large-group concepts I described in this chapter that are utilized to protect and maintain large-group identity.

In a regressed large group, political, legal, or traditional borders become highly psychologized and people, leaders, and official organizations become preoccupied with their protection. When a large group is in a regressed state, the personality and the internal world of the political leader assumes great importance concerning the manipulation (the "good" or the "bad") of what already exists within the large-group psychology. Later in this book I will examine such leader–follower interactions.

When large group progression takes place most members of the large group change their attitudes about the political or religious leader's political propaganda and feel comfortable to have freedom of speech, and to wonder what is moral and beautiful and how fantasy is different than reality. If a large-group regression had taken place after a scary conflict or an actual fight with another large group, when progression returns the previously regressed population can start noticing humane aspects of persons who were previously perceived as enemies.

CHAPTER THREE

Large-group identity
that develops in adulthood

During unofficial dialogues between representatives of opposing national and ethnic groups under the auspices of the Center for the Study of Mind and Human Interaction (CSMHI), these participants were defending their large-group identities which had developed in childhood. Following my two visits to Colombia during recent years where I learned more about the impact of guerrilla movements on society, and after the Finnish historian Jouni Suistola and I studied Al-Qaeda and the so-called Islamic State of Iraq and the Levant (ISIS) (Suistola & Volkan, 2017), I began paying more attention to large-group identities that develop in adulthood.

Employees of a huge international business corporation, or tens of thousands or millions of followers of a sports team, or members of an academic organization can be imagined as belonging to this type of large group. However, working for an international business organization or following a basketball team or sharing the same academic profession does not move people to drastically modify the core large-group identity they developed in childhood. On the other hand, guerrilla movements, such as Fuerzas Armadas Revolucionarias de Colombia (the Revolutionary Armed Forces of Colombia, FARC), and terrorist organizations, such as Al-Qaeda and ISIS, and some religious cults, such as Aum Shinrikyo and the Branch Davidians, truly represent large groups that evolve during adulthood and lead to their members losing their moral attitudes—the superego-imposed restrictions which are linked to the large-group identity they acquired as children. Such individuals' investments in their core large-group identities that had developed in childhood drastically change. They exaggerate selected aspects of their childhood large-group identities by holding on to a distinct nationalistic or religious belief. Alternatively, they become believers of ideas that were not available in their childhood environments. In short, they give up sharing overall sentiments with people who had the same core childhood large-group identity by making specific new selections that set them apart.

Belonging to this second type large-group identity in adulthood may even allow members to take part in mass suicides, as seen with followers of Peoples Temple in 1978 and Heaven's Gate in 1997. The members of these cults had not come from cultures where ritualistic suicides had occurred in the past, such as in the Samurai tradition in Japan. Belonging to a second type large-group identity also allows horrific sadistic acts to be committed against others, such as ISIS members cutting the throats of their "enemies" without hesitation. Members perceive their actions as a natural duty to protect or bring attention to their new large-group identity acquired in adulthood (Volkan, 2018b).

Jouni Suistola and I described how some large groups which evolve in adulthood also inflame specific chosen traumas and entitlement ideologies, and create time collapse and purification (Suistola & Volkan, 2017). For example, Al-Qaeda and ISIS reactivated Sunni Arab Muslim chosen trauma, the loss of the Caliphate and wished to replace it with glory. During the reign of Sultan Selim I (1512 to 1520), the Ottomans took over Syria and Egypt, and by 1517 the Arab Sunni Caliphates had come to an end. After the defeat of the Ottoman Empire and with the birth of modern Turkey, in 1923 the Caliphate—in a sense Sunni Islam's "papacy"—was abolished, and centuries of Islam's established leadership suddenly disappeared.

Al-Qaeda searched for a caliphate; ISIS declared itself as a caliphate. The late Abu Bakr al Baghdadi called himself a caliph (Caliph Ibrahim) and commander of ISIS. It is said that Caliph Ibrahim is descended from the tribe of the Prophet, the Quraysh, and ISIS used this to "legitimize" his claim as a caliph. I do not have in-depth information about this man's childhood and life in general.

Meanwhile starting a "caliphate" was perceived as a "container" for many frustrated individuals, as well as lone-wolf terrorists, and joining or following ISIS was a means to increase their self-esteem. The fact is that many who went to Syria to join ISIS were not religious practitioners; they were searching for a "tent" to cover up their personal identity problems or conflicts (Suistola &Volkan, 2017; Volkan, 2017a).

When studying large groups which develop in adulthood I also noted how some types of large-group regression in religious cults do not have direct links to the relationship with an opposing large group. Instead, they reflect the influence of the group's "new" identity. Treating women, even children, badly as if they are not at the level of men is one example of this.

CHAPTER FOUR

Psychology of decision-making and political leader–follower relationships

S ince it was introduced by Ludwig von Rochau in 1853, the concept of *realpolitik* has evolved to mean the rational evaluation and realistic assessment of options available to one's large group and its enemies without considering in-depth psychological processes. Realism dominated political thinking for the next century. During the Cold War years, realpolitik gave birth to what became known as *rational actor* models of politics and diplomacy. According to these models, political leaders and governments function like "rational" individuals.

The rational actor model was prevalent in political analysis in the United States during the height of the Cold War and it was even nicknamed the "American model" (Allison, 1971; Barner-Barry & Rosenwein, 1985). It was assumed that in an "exceptional" country like the United States political decision-making was purely logical and unaffected by psychological factors. Some American political analysts stated that other developed countries also used this model.

Although its very definition implied cool, rational, and clear thought process, the rational actor model actually made a number of working assumptions about human behavior. The first was that decision-makers had preferences and made choices based on rationally understood circumstances. Second, it assumed that variation of outcomes depended on the opportunities available to the decision-maker rather than on differences in the norms, roles, or cultures involved. The third assumption held that the state or political entity acted as a single, rational actor, and that modifications in personnel—including the political leader and members of the leader's entourage—did not come into play in the decision-making process (Achen & Snidal, 1989).

It was cognitive psychologists who recognized the shortcomings of rational actor models (see for example: Janis & Mann, 1977; Jervis, Lebow, & Stein, 1985; Rokeach, 1984). They began to examine how different political leaders used different dominant historical analogies in their decision-making. For example, they referred to President Dwight Eisenhower's decision not to intervene at Dien Bien Phu in 1954. Eisenhower's lesson from Korea was that the United States must not become involved in another distant land war. Yet, I thought, cognitive psychologists' contributions to leaders' decision-making theory, although important, were somewhat limited. Since cognitive psychologists primarily focused on conscious processes, the influence of unconscious processes was not truly taken into consideration.

Psychoanalysts were not interested in studying and writing about decision-making. There was a major exception. Leo Rangell who was twice president of the International Psychoanalytical Association (IPA) and also president of the American Psychoanalytic Association, described "a decision-making function of the ego" (1971, p. 431). Nine years later he would publish a book examining Richard Nixon's mind and his involvement in the Watergate scandal (Rangell, 1980).

Here is a summary of Rangell's theory of individual decision-making: He made reference to Freud's (1926d) concept of signal anxiety which foreshadows intrapsychic danger and initiates defensive operations. The aim of these defenses is to keep derivatives of impulses and/or painful affects from emerging into consciousness and/or actions. According to Rangell, before fully experiencing signal anxiety, the ego permits a small, controlled amount of impulse to discharge—a tiny test within the mind, to see whether the ego can allow the impulse full-blown expression.

When this test happens, an individual's superego responds to the trial discharge and causes the ego to produce anxiety. Like the impulse that initiated it, the level of this anxiety is small—below the level of signal anxiety. At this point, the ego must choose what to do next: allow the full discharge of the impulse or stop the impulse from being discharged. Rangell called this process "intrapsychic choice conflict." He wrote:

> The delineation of an intrapsychic choice conflict spells out a moment in intrapsychic life in which the human psyche is

confronted with the opportunity, and the necessity, to exercise its own directive potentials and to determine its own active course … Taken by itself, psychic determinism is incomplete, unless it is viewed in the context of the role played by the individual himself in controlling and shaping his own destiny. (1971, p. 440)

Rangell also described "a decision-making function of the ego" (p. 431) specifically designed to resolve the intrapsychic choice conflict, which is followed by action. The anxiety–choice–decision–action sequence he describes serves as the theoretical model for the psychoanalytic contribution to decision theory. All decision-making, whether it is about buying a house or engaging in an international conflict, involves planning. During this planning process the individual unconsciously scans "memories of previous psychic traumata, by which the utility of anticipated decisions is judged. The scope and security of predictions are thus enormously amplified by bringing into play previous experience and the entire sweep of the genetic past" (Rangell, 1971, p. 439).

Rangell told us that as a child matures into an adult, decision-making begins to involve increasingly sophisticated and conscious (secondary process) thinking. But, some of the problem-solving preceding it continues to take place largely on an unconscious level. Fixation and regression in the adult individual's mental life influence decision-making functions. When fixations and regressions are severe enough, the secondary process thinking involved in decision-making is inhibited.

During my involvement in international affairs my focus was on the impact of political leaders' decision-making on large groups. The founder and first president of the Turkish Republic of North Cyprus, Rauf Denktaş, was a friend of mine (Atik, 2019). I spent a considerable time with Jimmy Carter and a shorter time with Mikhail Gorbachev after their leaderships ended. Before becoming the president of Estonia Arnold Rüütel was a member of Estonia's team when the Center for the Study of Mind and Human Interaction (CSMHI) facilitators conducted years-long unofficial dialogues between Estonians and Russians. I visited Yasser Arafat when he was running the Palestinian Liberation Organization (PLO) in exile from Tunis. I observed aspects of leader–follower psychology through these leaders' verbalized thought processes and actions. I also examined local people's stories about dictators Enver Hoxha and Nicolae Ceaușescu in Albania and Romania respectively after the deaths of these dictators.

Sigmund Freud, in his exchange with Albert Einstein (Freud, 1933b), stated that all human beings are either leaders or followers. Obviously, the latter constitute by far the majority. The leader–follower relationship is a two-way street: it is influenced and determined by the leader's personality and by the followers' shared conscious and unconscious wishes and needs (Volkan, 1980, 1988, 2014a). The movement of traffic on both sides of the street is dependent on many factors. The two-way traffic may become congested due to the psychological makeup of the leader or due to the shared conscious and unconscious needs of their followers. To an extent these needs center upon the issues related to large-group psychology in its own right.

Based on his experience in President John F. Kennedy's administration and his observations of Kennedy and other political figures, political science professor James MacGregor Burns (1984) identified two types of political leaders: *transactional* and *transforming*. The transactional leader acts according to political polls and national climate, and follows existing societal sentiments, becoming a spokesperson for them. Such a leader thrives on bargaining, manipulating, accommodating, and compromising within a given system. In a stable democracy that is not experiencing economic, political, or military stress, the personality of a transactional leader typically is not of critical importance.

A transforming leader "transcends and even seeks to reconstruct the political system, rather than simply operating within it" (Burns, 1984, p. 16).

In Burns' reference to transforming leaders we catch an echo of the description of charismatic leaders by Maximilian Weber (1925). Weber stated that charismatic leaders come to power at times of crisis within their large groups. He observed that the charismatic leader is obeyed by virtue of personal trust in him and his revelation, his heroism, or his exemplary qualities so far as they fall within the scope of the individual's belief in his charisma. It is suggested that the charismatic leader has both paternal and maternal characteristics; charismatic leaders provide a "total" parent image for their followers (Abse & Jessner, 1961; Volkan & Itzkowitz, 1984).

The formal and informal systems of "checks and balances" in a well-functioning democracy prevent a leader's personality—his or her habitual ways of behaving and feeling due to personal emotional problems, as well as positive adaptations—from exerting undue influence over government and the governed. Even a transforming leader will not cause fundamental changes in such a society. Under certain circumstances, however, the personality of a transforming political leader can be a major factor in creating new and drastic societal and political processes.

I have defined transforming leaders—who dedicate themselves to changing the followers' external and internal worlds in order to lift up their individual self-esteem and to modify their large-group identity—as reparative and destructive (Volkan, 2004). Reparative leaders achieve these tasks, or try to achieve them, without humiliating, hurting, or killing groups of people who are not his or her followers. By the term destructive, I refer to leaders who resort to mass humiliation or destruction of the Other.

In the next chapter I will focus on political leaders' involvement in political propaganda.

CHAPTER FIVE

Political propaganda

A simple definition of political propaganda, in its widest sense, would encompass any communication and manipulation from a source of political authority that is directed to its followers and its opposition at home and/or abroad, as well as to those who might be described as "neutrals;" its aim is to further the propagandist's wishes and ideas. First, I will give a brief history of political propaganda.

The historical precursor to political propaganda may be the tribal battle cries of earlier times "meant to encourage one's own group, frighten the foe, and impress those who did not participate" (Kris, 1943, p. 382). The ancient war cry, called *alala*, accompanied by nonverbal symbols such as banners and uniforms, is said to have been a significant psychological factor for the Greeks and for their enemies. The ancient Roman armies used shouts and accompanying trumpet blasts, called *clamor*, and later adapted the Teutonic battle cry, *barditus*. "Tacitus describes it as an explosion of raucous sounds, made more prolonged and more resounding by pressing the shield against the mouth" (Chakotin, 1939, p. 34). Beginning as a murmur, it would steadily increase into a roar, rousing the soldiers to intense excitement. And the battle cry of a more recent empire, the Ottoman, was simply their God's name, as if their battles were sanctioned by God and as if any Ottoman soldier killed in battle would be taken care of by Him. Ottoman janissaries shouted "Allah! Allah!" as their colorful marching band, the *Mehter*, provided a background of musical excitement.

As human history proceeded, other means of influencing feeling and behavior and generating support for political decisions in times of conflict superseded the battle cry, and the use of such methods in peacetime as well as in war became more common too. Interestingly, the appearance of propaganda (from the Latin "to propagate" or "to sow") in its broadest sense paralleled the elaboration of forms of religious, social, and political organization. Garth Jowett and Victoria O'Donnell (1992) describe how the concept of "propagating" ideas lost its neutrality: in 1622, *Sacra Conregatio de Propaganda Fide* (the "sacred congregation for propagating the faith" of the Roman Catholic Church) was established by the Vatican; the term "propaganda" thus became pejorative in Protestant Western Europe because it was associated with the project of spreading Catholicism in the New World at the expense of and in opposition to the "reformed" faiths.

When I was an inaugural Yitzhak Rabin fellow in Israel in 2000 I had a chance to spend time with the late Bernard Lewis, a Princeton University historian specializing in oriental studies, who was also a guest in Israel at that time. At a meeting at the Rabin Center, Bernard Lewis (2000) suggested that political propaganda, in its modern sense, did not begin until after the 1789 French Revolution. Before the Revolution, he argued, there was essentially no meaningful contact between the rulers and the ordinary people. Those in power had no need to communicate with or to manipulate the public—they simply ruled. After the seismic shift of the French Revolution, however, rulers began to need political propaganda in order to secure at least the appearance of consent from those they governed.

Earlier, historian Harold Lasswell, a pioneer in the study of psycho-social warfare who was interested in studying history from a psychoanalytic angle, had suggested that the "discovery of propaganda by both the man in the street and the man in the study" took place during World War I (1914–1918). "The layman had previously lived in a world where there was no common name for the deliberate forming of attitudes by the manipulation of words (and word substitutes)" (Lasswell, 1938, p. v). By the end of World War I, communication technologies had drastically improved, enabling direct contact with the public on an unprecedented scale. Besides printed material, telegrams and the wireless were routinely available to influence the masses. The Nazi propaganda of World War II created a situation where the "Aryan" identity of the German people was built up while millions of Jews and also others were dehumanized and killed. In Nazi propaganda the emphasis was on maintaining the Führer's omnipotence. The leader's own internal psychological processes, supported by his followers, dominated the malignant political and sociological outcomes.

The ever more rapid proliferation of communication technologies in the last several decades has, predictably, diversified the means and methods of political manipulation and influence. The main focus of propaganda dealing with large-group identity issues in the current international arena is to establish a psychological border between one's own group and the neighbor group and within the same country between those who like the political leader and those who do not. Atrocities may be committed in the service of maintaining this psychological border.

Donald Trump frequently uses Twitter and makes political remarks, attacks his opponents, and often makes false statements. I believe that we can name what he is doing as a "new" form of "propaganda." His references to an "invasion" by unwanted Others and his focus on building a physical/psychological border between the USA and Mexico enhance a sense of victimization and increase a desire for purification by those who agree with Donald Trump.

A destructive transforming leader's propaganda machine can be seen to follow five steps in this process:

1. Reactivating a chosen trauma;
2. Enhancing a shared sense of victimization within the large group;
3. Increasing a sense of "we-ness" by returning to a chosen glory;
4. Devaluing and dehumanizing the Other; and
5. Creating a sense of entitlement for revenge. Through these five steps, an atmosphere is created in which large-group members feel entitled to humiliate or even destroy the current Other and purify their large-group identity.

CHAPTER SIX

Applying the tree model
and large-group consultations

There is a need to study the situation of each large group from many angles in order to find specific elements in large-group processes, to understand their underlying meanings, and then begin to plan psychologically informed political/societal or diplomatic strategies for inducing progression within the large group or two or more large groups in conflict. In this chapter first I will provide a summary of a method I have called the Tree Model that provides such strategies and their application. Descriptions of detailed applications of the Tree Model have been published earlier (Atik, 2019; Volkan, 1999a, 2006, 2013).

The Tree Model

The Tree Model is based on the assumption that large-group identity issues described above are involved in every aspect of the political, economic, social, legal, or military relationships between large groups, when the groups are under stress or engaged in protracted conflicts. In such situations, psychological issues contaminate the real-world issues and create resistances to peaceful and adaptive solutions. These psychological "poisons," both conscious and unconscious, must be removed before constructive communication and negotiation can take place between opposing large groups and before the easing of tensions can be institutionalized and maintained for the long term.

The Tree Model methodology grew out of the experiences of the Center for the Study of Mind and Human Interaction (CSMHI) faculty members individually and as a team in a variety of long-term projects in the field. It is a multi-year process with three components: 1) Psycho-political assessment of the problems (roots of the tree); 2) Psycho-political dialogues (the trunk of the tree); and 3) Institution building (branches of the tree).

Psycho-political assessment of the problems (roots of the tree)

Before travelling to a particular country or region to begin work, CSMHI's interdisciplinary team studied the history and culture of the antagonist groups, collected information on the current situation, and identified problems. From the beginning, it was clear that interdisciplinary collaboration was needed. For example, even though the historian on the CSMHI team might not be an expert in the particular country, he brought a way of thinking that contributed to understanding the information gathered. Clinicians brought insights about the mental images of historical events. Presidents of the countries, rectors of universities, mayors, taxi drivers, teachers, and regional experts were consulted, as were the local newspapers when available.

Hot places

I use this term to describe a physical location that individually and collectively induces immediate and intense feelings among the members of an ethnic, religious, national, or ideological large group. It typically is a place where people have been recently killed and/or humiliated by Others. Hot places induce shared active or passive feelings of sadness, rage, and victimization, a desire for revenge, and other emotions associated with complicated grief or mourning. Listening to various individuals at hot places is to large-group psychology what recounting dreams is to an individual undergoing psychoanalysis.

Estonians were naturally euphoric after regaining their independence from the Soviet Union in 1991. But CSMHI was able to uncover other less obvious aspects of the Estonian outlook through intensive interviews with a wide range of Estonians and through visits to hot places such as the former Soviet nuclear submarine base at Paldiski. We found that Estonians suffered from an underlying anxiety of "disappearing" as an ethnic group, of ceasing to exist. Their unusual chosen trauma of living under the rule of other nations was inflamed. While there were plenty of real-world issues to attend to, the perception that Estonia would "disappear" caused resistance to policies for integrating the Russians and non-Estonian Russian speakers (one third of the population) living in Estonia. If Estonian and Russian "blood" were to "mix," the uniqueness of the Estonian people in their newly independent country might not survive. Our diagnosis then indicated the need to help Estonians differentiate real issues from fantasized fears so that they could deal more adaptively with the integration of the Russians and Russian-speakers living in Estonia.

Psychopolitical dialogues (the trunk of the tree)

After diagnosis, the next step is to convene a series of psycho-political dialogues among members of the opposing large groups (or within a single large group if there is internal fragmentation). Ten to fifteen participants from each side are selected, ideally influential officials and policy-makers, meeting in a strictly unofficial capacity. We meet for four days at a time, several times a year, these discussion groups becoming a "laboratory" for what is going on in the large groups they represent. In this laboratory, the facilitators can see and help identify the events that are activated to protect the large-group identities. Some of these events are hostile and impede rational progress toward peace, recovery, and coexistence.

During the first day of an initial meeting between influential Turks and Greeks discussing their conflicts over the Aegean Sea and Cyprus, frustrating emotions were high as participants expressed their perceptions of the "enemy." That evening at dinner, participants enjoyed each other as "friends." While attending the next morning's meeting, a Greek participant spoke of her confusion: She had felt hurt and angry during the day and friendly at the dinner. How was she supposed to behave? The facilitators then helped her see how her personal identity and large-group identity are on a continuum and that, during the meeting, she had inevitably become a spokesperson of her large group, while at dinner, her individual identity held sway. She and the other Greek and Turkish participants were asked to let themselves wear the canvas of their large-group identity as their garment during the meetings. This would be the only way to observe the psychodynamics of Turkish–Greek interactions at close range. In other words, CSMHI did not try to force an emotionally civil atmosphere at the meetings, but rather aimed to allow emotions, including anxiety and anger, to be expressed at an appropriate level. The clinicians on the CSMHI team try to ensure that such emotions remain useful for insights into the conflict, and that the emotions neither degenerate to destructive levels nor are so denied that only detached intellectual statements are made during the meeting.

The psycho-political dialogues are central to the success of the Tree Model. There are certain key patterns of behavior and strategies that characterize the process of psycho-political dialogues. They evolve and are repeated during each four-day meeting as well as in a larger process over the entire two- to three-year series. Below I will describe them briefly without providing in-depth examples of each pattern and strategy. Detailed examples from the American Psychiatric Association sponsored Arab–Israeli dialogues and CSMHI's work with representatives of other opposing large groups are available in my previous publications (Volkan, 1988, 1997, 1999a, 2006, 2013).

Displacement onto a mini-conflict

Sometimes, at the outset of a dialogue meeting, a disruptive situation evolves abruptly and absorbs the attention and energy of all participants. Such a situation is usually marked with a sense of urgency, yet the content of this "crisis" is essentially insignificant in comparison to the salient aspects of the large-group conflict for which the dialogue meeting has been organized. I call such situations "mini-conflicts." For example, during a meeting between high-level Israelis and Arabs, an Arab delegate demanded a minute's silence in memory of a fallen Arab who was an obvious enemy of the Israelis. I asked everybody to stand up and silently, in their minds, honor whoever they wished to honor. The mini-conflict was resolved.

A mini-conflict is much like the masques that precede an Elizabethan tragedy, which provide condensed and symbolically suggestive treatments of what will be explored dramatically later in the play. " ... any leader of a facilitating team should heed it carefully, within the limits of reality and neutrality, and resolve it in a spirit of compromise in order to establish the tone of the dialogue" (Volkan, 2013, p. 58).

The echo phenomenon

During psycho-political dialogues, I saw the shadow of some recent military or political development fall over the work group, further igniting emotions that exacerbate resistance to adaptive situations. I call this an echo phenomenon. It then becomes necessary to acknowledge and assimilate this shadow and its meaning for both sides before positive negotiation can continue.

Competition to express chosen traumas and chosen glories

At unofficial dialogue meetings, the compulsion to list grievances, especially at the outset, seems involuntary. Members of opposing large groups in dialogue frequently enter into a competition to list historical grievances including chosen traumas and past triumphs, including chosen glories. There is no empathy for the other side's losses and injuries and no appreciation for the other side's glories. The task of the facilitating team, therefore, is to serve as models for empathic listening.

Projection and projective identification

Members of one large group in conflict may attempt to define their identity through externalizing unwanted parts of themselves onto the enemy, projecting their unwanted thoughts, perceptions, and wishes. For example, it is not *we* who are troublemakers, but *them*. Often projections onto the opposing group reflected a clear "us" and "them" dichotomy of rigid positions: we are "good," they are "bad." During a dialogue series, we noted how projections can also involve a more complex relationship between representatives of the two opposing large groups in a pattern similar to the mechanism of projective identification that, as Melanie Klein (1946) stated, psychoanalysts see in individual patients. At the dialogue series one team may project onto the other their own wishes for how the opposing side should think, feel, or behave. The first team then identifies with the Other that houses their projections—this Other is perceived as actually acting in accordance with the expectations of the former. In effect, one team becomes the "spokesperson" for the other team, and since this process takes place unconsciously, the first team actually believes their remarks about the enemy. However, the resulting "relationship" is not real since it is based on the processes of only one party. The facilitating team interpret or interfere with the development of projective identification, since once it develops, the reality of perceptions is compromised.

The accordion phenomenon

The CSMHI team observed that after some airing of chosen traumas and chosen glories, or their derivatives, and when more empathic communication began, the representatives of opposing large groups experienced a rapprochement. This closeness was then followed by a sudden withdrawal from one another and then again by closeness. The pattern was repeated numerous times. I liken this to the playing of an accordion—squeezing together and then pulling apart. Initial distancing is a defensive maneuver to keep aggressive attitudes and feelings in check, since, if the opponents were to come together, they might harm one another—at least in fantasy— or in turn become targets of retaliation. When opposing teams are confined together in one room, sharing conscious efforts for peace, sometimes they must deny their aggressive feelings as they press together in a kind of illusory union. When this becomes oppressive, it feels dangerous, and distancing occurs again. The most realistic discussions take place after the facilitating team has allowed the accordion to play for a while, until the squeezing and distancing becomes less extreme.

Minor differences

We have found that minor differences between opposing groups are often psychologically harder to deal with than major differences, such as language or religion. When minor differences become resistances, the facilitating team try to enhance and verify each group's identity, so that the minor differences remain minor.

Personal stories

Participants in dialogues invariably bring up personal stories pertaining to the large-group conflict at hand. Initially, personal stories often reflected an "us" and "them" (or "me" and "them") psychology in a black and white manner. This is similar to the mechanism of splitting that clinicians see among certain patients who divide and experience themselves, intimate others, and their mental images as either all "good" or all "bad." As empathy evolves, however, stories begin to include ambivalences. To have ambivalence is to begin to acknowledge the other's identity as a total being who is both similar and dissimilar, liked and disliked; the other begins to become more human.

Symbolizing the conflict and "playing" with it

The CSMHI team noted that a symbol or metaphor that represents important aspects of the conflict would emerge from within the dialogue after the same representatives of the opposing large groups had met on several occasions each year for two or three years. For example, the weaker party called itself a mouse while referring to the stronger enemy as an elephant. Then, the participants began to "play" with this metaphor, to kick it around like a ball. As this play continued, poisonous emotions began to disappear, and laughter often accompanied the banter. Serious realistic discussion of issues could then ensue. (It is important to note that the facilitating team should *not* introduce or fabricate a metaphor or "toy" for the participants to play with—it must be created or provided by the participants themselves.)

One positive side effect of the participants' creating and playing with symbols and metaphors during the dialogue series is the transformation of large-group *protosymbols* (things that become what they represent) into symbols. In war-like situations, large groups' cultural amplifiers are perceived by one or both sides as protosymbols, not merely symbols but real. To turn them back into symbols is a sign of progress.

Time expansion

When chosen traumas and their derivatives are reactivated, the emotions and perceptions pertaining to them are felt as if the trauma occurred recently—they become fused with emotions and perceptions pertaining to the present and are even projected into the future. Understandably, this time collapse complicates attempts to resolve the conflicts at hand. To counteract this phenomenon and to encourage a time expansion, CSMHI facilitators allow discussions to take place concerning the chosen trauma itself and participants' personal traumas pertaining to the large-group conflict. Then feelings and issues about the past are distanced and separated from current problems, and more intense realistic negotiations take place.

New ways of thinking

Based on observation and understanding of the above processes as they take place during the dialogues, the CSMHI facilitating team intervene and guide the discussions to weaken or remove the psychological obstacles and to enable the participants to communicate more realistically with each other. In time, they begin to develop creative ideas for applying and promoting these new ways of thinking and interacting.

Institution building (branches of the tree)

The third component of the Tree Model involves transferring the insights from the dialogues into concrete actions affecting the large groups involved. In collaboration with the dialogue participants and local contacts trained in the CSMHI methodology, the CSMHI team seek to prevent stagnation or slipping backwards by institutionalizing the progress that has been made. The local contact group includes clinicians trained to work in the societies involved at a grass roots level to create models for coexistence or collaboration.

In Estonia, for example, within the three years following the psycho-political dialogues, we were able to build model coexistence projects in two villages where the population is half Estonian and half Russian. We also created a model to promote integration among Estonian and Russian schoolchildren and influenced the language examination required for Russians to become Estonian citizens (Volkan, 1997, 2006, 2013). The most important task here was to "teach" people at the grass roots level to gain political power, and to help local contact groups to evolve as effective NGOs.

Consultations

The Tree Model was offered as a methodology for a new type of preventive or corrective unofficial diplomacy carried out systematically by a neutral third party. After I retired from the University of Virginia and after the Center for the Study of Mind and Human Interaction (CSMHI) was closed in 2005 the Tree Model was never applied to an international problem or problems within the same large group. I was invited to consult with authorities or influential individuals at various places of the world, such as Kuwait, Malaysia, Turkey, Colombia, and try to understand both conscious and unconscious issues of the large-group processes they were dealing with (Volkan, 2013). What my decades-long work with the CSMHI team taught me was most useful in suggesting methods for adjusting to recent traumas at the hand of the Other, finding ways for peaceful coexistence, and preventing the emergence of societal conflicts.

The most recent request, in 2019, to help with a large-group problem really surprised me. I was asked to supervise two individuals who were selected by the UK government to go to the Pitcairn Islands and discuss the future of the people living there. The Pitcairn Islands, a British territory, are in the middle of the Pacific Ocean and they are famous as the place where, in the 1790s, the mutineers from the ship HMS *Bounty* (along with nine Tahitian men and twelve Tahitian women whom they "kidnapped") ran to and inhabited. Today forty-five people, mostly descendants of the original mutineers, live on the Pitcairn Islands. Her Majesty's Government posts a small group of officials (administrator, police officer, health worker, teacher) on this location.

A child sex scandal rocked the territory in 2004 which ended up with six men being convicted and imprisoned on the Pitcairn Islands. The purpose of the two individuals was to assist the islanders in developing a strategy for a sustainable community or another strategy if a sustainable population were not possible. My supervision was helpful in acknowledging how a shared *Bounty identity* is very valued on the Pitcairn Islands. It is holding the small population back from addressing their current realities and challenges. Many in the Pitcairn community worry about losing the core aspects of their identity. The two individuals have succeeded in starting a process to deal with the Pitcairn Islands problem.

International dialogue initiative (IDI)

In Chapter One, I wrote that, in 2008, I founded the International Dialogue Initiative (IDI). My initial aim was to bring together representatives from different countries to examine international tensions, especially between the Middle East and the West. With the help of another psychoanalyst, Lord John Alderdice, who was then located in Northern Ireland and who had been a key figure in creating peace in that part of the world, I selected influential individuals from Germany, Iran, Israel, Russia, Turkey, the United Kingdom, the United States, and the West Bank as the IDI members. We began to meet twice a year, each time for three days.

Today the IDI is an independent organization, with charitable status in the United States (www.internationaldialogueinitiative.com). All original members of the IDI continue to meet. For me these meetings have become a symbol of a wishful development that clearly illustrates when people from opposing large groups talk, they do not kill each other.

Under the leadership of the present president of the IDI, Gerard Fromm, PhD, who was the director of the Erik Erikson Institute for Education and Research at the Austen Riggs Center, "Volkan Scholars," selected from different countries, began to attend the IDI meetings.

In 2017 the IDI began to offer a two-day training workshop that teaches large-group psychology in its own right, provides opportunities for the participants to reflect on large-group identity in their personal lives, and examines different cases in an effort to apply large-group psychology principles to actual work on social conflict. During our first three training programs that took place in Vienna, Austria and Geneva, Switzerland, the attendees from the United States, Europe, the Middle East, China, and South Sudan included management consultants, educators, conflict resolution practitioners, and psychoanalysts.

CHAPTER SEVEN

Cherry hospital:
personal observations on racism

An examination of large-group psychology in its own right includes a study of racism. Racism is discrimination based on a belief that there is a specific biological inequality between races that is reflected in the deficient personality, intellect, and culture of members of the "lower" races. Modern racist theories stress a wider, more anthropological basis, such as religion, language, family and social structure, and value systems as justification to keep races separate and perceive them unbendable. There has been confusion between racism and ethnic hatreds and the concepts of race relative to ethnic identity. The confusing overlap between racism and ethnocentrism can be ignored if they are both viewed as forms of hostile or malignant prejudice.

When I was a child in Cyprus, I was aware of the differences between ethnic groups on the island. During the deadly interethnic conflict, including the murder of my former roommate and imprisonment of my family in an enclave for eleven years, sometimes I would feel deep hostility against Cypriot Greeks. But they were human beings as Cypriot Turks were human beings: they did not belong to a "lower" race. As time has passed, I no longer have such hostility and enjoy the company of my Greek friends.

I recall that during my childhood and youth I only saw three individuals of African descent who were Cypriot Turks. One of them, an elementary school teacher, was a friend of my sisters. The second one was a man who would ride on his bicycle in front of our house and say "Hi" to me and my friends playing in the street. The third one was a much younger kid than me who belonged to our Boy Scout group. All of them were Cypriot Turks with black skin. Today hundreds of students from Africa attend several North Cyprus universities.

After I became a psychiatrist, I learned that a child begins to perceive color as early as three months of age and to discriminate colors by one year. In 1970 Marjorie McDonald wrote about *skin color anxiety*. She stated that a young child who is confronted by a person of a different color will register the difference and will experience anxiety. I do not recall experiencing skin color anxiety when I was a child and also after I arrived in the USA where I learned what hostile racism is. In this chapter I will describe my personal observations of hostile racism and its psychological impact on me.

While I was going through my psychiatric residency training from 1958 to 1961 at the University of North Carolina, I received a little financial support from the State of North Carolina. In turn, I agreed to work for two years at a state mental hospital as soon as I finished my training in late 1961. I was assigned to Cherry Hospital in Goldsboro, North Carolina as a new psychiatrist. When this hospital was opened in August 1880 its name was "Asylum for Colored Insane." It was one of the first mental hospitals for only African Americans.

In 1845 Francis Stribling, MD, a leader of the Association of Medical Superintendents of American Institutions for the Insane (which later became the American Psychiatric Association) wrote a report on "Colored persons of unsound mind." He stated:

> No provisions having been made here for the comfortable accommodation of this class of patients, we have never found it practicable to admit them, although occasional applications have been made to us on behalf of free blacks and frequently of slaves. We will simply remark that for many reasons it would be desirable that an institution for colored persons should be entirely distinct from those occupied by insane whites. (Davis, 2019, p. 9)

The first mental hospital, a temporary one, for African Americans was opened in 1870 near Richmond, Virginia. The permanent one became available in 1885 near Petersburg, Virginia (Davis, 2019), five years after the "Asylum for Colored Insane" in Goldsboro, North Carolina was established.

There have been several name changes for the hospital in Goldsboro. In 1959 the name became Cherry Hospital in honor of Governor R. Gregg Cherry. I ended up working at Cherry Hospital for nearly two years when it was still a treatment facility only for African American patients. Later, after I moved to Charlottesville, Virginia, I visited the hospital near Petersburg as a consultant on many occasions. By then, this hospital was no longer only for African American patients.

As a young man, as the saying goes, I had come to America to find "gold." For me "gold" was not defined in financial terms, but by a wish to expand my mind and embrace high human ideals. Instead, in my very first job in the United States, at Cherry Hospital, I found myself in an environment lacking in human dignity. I was about to see at close range hostile racism and its influence on people who were subjected to it.

As I recall now, in the early 1960s, at Cherry Hospital there was not a single white physician who was born in the United States. The care of African American mental patients was given completely to immigrant white doctors, many of whom had escaped from countries under communist rule such as Lithuania or Hungary and were traumatized. We were given books and papers to read in order to understand the psychological problems of our patients, thousands of them at Cherry Hospital. There were many references to a type of delusion common among African American patients: a delusion of being white. Most writers were following the lead of John Lind (1914a, 1914b), a forensic psychiatrist, who had coined the term "color complex" of the "American Negro." A product of his time, Lind believed that the psychological processes of African Americans were less complex than those of Caucasians and conceived of African Americans as "little children" and their dreams as direct fulfillment of their wishes. Lind concluded that African Americans' dreams suggested their simple desire to be white, an interpretation he found further support for in the delusions of the African American patients he studied.

There were many papers and books by other writers focusing on African American patients' "color-complex" stating how African American children, after coming into contact with white children, begin to measure their personal worth by degrees of proximity to white complexion or other Caucasian features and that most African Americans with mental issues exhibit color denial and a wish to be white (Brody, 1963; Charles, 1942; Dai, 1953; Goodman, 1952; Kennedy, 1952; Myers & Yochelson, 1948; Vitols, Walters, & Keeler, 1963). Our African American patients' domineering mothers and absent fathers were blamed for their mental problems. There was no serious consideration expressed about the role of hostile racism in the development of African American patients' symptoms. It was only in the late 1960s and early 1970s that prominent African American psychiatrists, Charles Pinderhughes and Charles Wilkerson, began publishing papers on the experience of being a reservoir for white Americans' externalizations of unwanted aspects or thoughts (Pinderhughes, 1969; Wilkerson, 1970). These scholars also exposed myths by showing, for example, that all impoverished children were prone to fail in school, not just black children.

My first assignment at Cherry Hospital was to look after 100 patients in a locked ward. The first time I entered this ward I noticed that I was the only white person there. As African American attendants walked me down a long hallway to show me around, at one point a huge man, a patient, tried to attack me. The attendants restrained him and I was not hurt, but it was very scary. Then I noticed that the attendants were smiling. They told me that the patient who tried to harm me always became "crazy and wild" whenever he saw a white person. They wanted to show this to me in order to warn me not to go near him alone. While their explanation relayed their concern for my welfare, I slowly began to think of the possibility that these African American attendants had set me up to be frightened. I had to be frightened by an African American as their way of showing me indirectly their unspoken frustration that a young white person was assigned to be their boss.

In those days there was a morning routine at Cherry Hospital. About 100 patients would receive electric shock therapy. The patients would line up two by two and wait to enter the room where they were restrained on a stretcher. Wires would be attached to their forehead and an attendant would put a piece of cloth in their mouth in order to prevent them from biting their tongue while convulsing. No anesthetics were given. A white doctor would push a button to produce the electricity. I, too, was "ordered" to give electric shock therapy; otherwise I would lose my job. One day I clearly associated the line of patients waiting to be electrically shocked with lines of Jewish people I had seen in films being guided to gas chambers. I felt shame and guilt.

A man with two birthmarks

In my first position as a psychiatrist I also noticed some African American patients' preoccupation with skin color. For example, a twenty-nine-year-old patient had some de-pigmented skin on his forehead, a spot about two inches in diameter. He was told that his mother had drunk "sweet milk" when she was pregnant, but while she was still thirsty for more milk, she rubbed her forehead with her hand. Supposedly because of this action, the patient was born with de-pigmented skin on the forehead. From early childhood on, the patient had the nickname of "The White Spot." As a child he struggled with ambivalent feelings about his leukoderma. At times he washed it with milk, as he was told by an old African American woman that washing the spot with milk would make it disappear. From his childhood on, he was teased about having a white father.

The patient had another birthmark above his right knee. In contrast to his "white spot," this second birthmark was of deeper pigmentation and looked darker than the patient's skin. He named the second birthmark as his "black spot." The two birthmarks represented his fantasized "white blood' and his "black identity" respectively.

The patient was a child of a promiscuous mother who had died when the patient was eleven years old. The patient never knew his father and this facilitated his fantasy of being half white. He was admitted to Cherry Hospital for having "spells," some kind of convulsive seizure, while looking at the full moon. He had his first spell during the first anniversary of being kicked out of his home by his African American wife after five years of marriage. He kept a calendar which showed the pictures of the changing moon.

I helped this patient to wonder about his preoccupation with the moon. He recalled hearing a legend about the moon when he was about five or six years old. He had heard that there was a white man on the moon who was putting fire on bushes on the moon and this made the full moon shine. As an adult, intellectually he never believed in this kind of legend, but now realized that all his life he had been looking at the full moon to see a man (the shape of a man) on it. Before his convulsive spells certain satellites were sent into space, and the patient had been told that a Russian (a white "enemy" man) had already landed on the moon.

Even though I was an inexperienced young psychiatrist I managed to help this patient to associate the moon with his "white spot" and a fantasized white father who had rejected him and who belonged to those who had seen him as inferior, and his "black spot" as something coming from his African American mother. He told me how, since his adolescence, he had never showed his "black spot" to anyone except his ex-wife. After he was rejected by his ex-wife/mother figure, psychologically speaking, he had turned his attention to a fantasized "white father," whom he perceived as an enemy. The patient showed me his "black spot" without being asked to do so. Then he watched the full moon one night without having a "spell." He was discharged from Cherry Hospital after spending three months there.

Slowly my experiences at Cherry Hospital led me to realize that most patients' "wish" to be white was accompanied by their anxiety about the idea of bearing white blood. I realized that these patients were both identifying with their oppressors and denying the pain of being reservoirs for the "bad" elements those oppressors had consigned to them, elements such as intellectual inferiority. Much later, when I came up with the tent metaphor describing large-group identity, I described how the tent's canvas has stains of mud thrown on it by the Other with hostile racism or ethnocentrism.

After psychoanalysts began studying how Jewish Holocaust survivors transmitted trauma from one generation to the next, we were warned not to ignore race, color, and trauma in psychoanalysis (Adams, 1996). The ancestors of African Americans endured 244 years of slavery and nearly a century of institutionalized terrorism. A psychoanalyst, Maurice Apprey (1996, 1998), originally from Ghana, concludes that "black-on-black crime" in the United States and situations like adolescent pregnancies among African Americans are related to slavery. As decades passed, the victimized group forgot who the original enemy was.

A "reenactment" of the slavery period of American history

During my second year at Cherry Hospital, I was assigned to work with patients in a building on a farm next to the hospital grounds—a place called the "Farm House"—that served as a kind of "laboratory" in which to observe a "reenactment" of the slavery period of American history. In the early 1960s there was land of 2,300 acres next to Cherry Hospital known as Cherry Farm which included fruit trees, an apple orchard, vegetables, and sugarcane, with livestock consisting of hogs, chickens, turkeys, and cows. The farm supplied the hospital's requirement of milk, eggs, pork, and 70 percent of the hospital's beef. The food at Cherry Hospital was excellent. Often, I would meet with other immigrant physicians and their families for dinner. They mostly talked about their relatives left behind; there was not much interest in speaking about our patients.

There were fifty male patients in their twenties or thirties living in the Farm House. When I entered there for the first time, I noticed that all of them looked physically very healthy. It was visiting hour, and I noticed many mothers, wives, or friends and relatives socializing with the young patients. There were also many children and a great deal of noise and laughter. The place did not look like a usual mental hospital, and I felt as if I was witnessing families on a Sunday picnic.

Before coming to the Farm House I imagined that the patients would benefit from working on the Cherry Farm as they would be involved in a kind of occupational therapy. I was shocked when I noticed the presence of a white American man, the chief attendant in charge of the Farm House, watching over the patients' get-together with their families. He was wearing boots and carrying a whip in his hand, looking like a lion tamer. When I introduced myself to him as the patients' new "doctor," he did not pay much attention to me. I was like an unimportant visitor to his plantation.

I began meeting and talking with each patient individually in the Farm House. The man wearing boots and carrying a whip did not mind my doing so as long as I would not keep his "slaves" away from their work on the farm too long. I noticed that almost all of the patients shared a common "delusion." It was not a "wish" to be white. They considered themselves as "Bucks." I had no idea what a "Buck" was, but soon learned that during slavery, young and virile slaves called "Bucks" were assigned to impregnate slave women in order to increase the slave population. I then understood that the patients at the farm shared a defensive adaptation. It was as if they were living during slave times and were working at a plantation under a white overseer with boots and a whip. They were trying to cover up their helplessness and humiliation by "believing" they were selected for their sexual superiority and breeding purposes. When I saw them with their families and friends, they were indeed behaving like "Bucks." (For more information on "Bucks," see: Andrews & Fenton, 2001; Fogel & Engerman, 1995; Follett, 2003).

Poems by four African American youngsters
who faced sudden desegregation

While I was working at Cherry Hospital, "desegregation" came to North Carolina. What happens to people of color in a situation like this? One day they are not allowed the "privilege" of sitting next to a white person, and overnight the law allows them to do so? What happens to the traumatized self after the discriminating laws are thrown out?

One day I was told that four African American youngsters had been admitted to Cherry Hospital suffering from "acute schizophrenia." When I met and spoke with them, I realized that their "schizophrenia" was due to their finding themselves suddenly in a desegregated situation. When a new Juvenile Evaluation Center was built in North Carolina, both white and African American male and female teenagers were transferred there from other segregated locations. The new center was fully desegregated except for the sleeping quarters. The fact that the white Americans and African Americans had to sleep separately stood as a reminder of the difference between the two races. Dancing between them was allowed. The four boys were sent to Cherry Hospital because of their confusion at finding themselves next to white boys and, even more disconcerting, close to white girls.

In the Cherry Hospital setting I could not find time to learn details of these four youngsters' lives. The oldest one, James, was sixteen and a half years old. He came from a section of North Carolina which at that time was known for bootlegging activities and juvenile delinquency. He was the next to the oldest among ten siblings. His father was not home most of the time, since he worked in another state and contributed financial support for the family. The patient, being one of the oldest, was left for the most part to make his own decisions. At times he was carried to the woods by adults to help to make illegally distilled whiskey. He saw the world as angry and threatening. He was sent to the "Negro training school" for African American male children because he was carrying a knife. Later he was transferred to the new desegregated Juvenile Evaluation Center. At this location he became very suspicious about white persons and was combative. He was diagnosed as having schizophrenia and was admitted to Cherry Hospital.

Nat was sixteen years old and an illegitimate child of a promiscuous mother. Until he was five, he lived in a rural area with his mother, a younger sister, and a man he called "father." At this time the family moved to a neighboring city leaving the man behind. I sensed that Nat was angry at the mother who caused his separation from the man who was left behind. His mother interfered in the youngster's masculine identification process. Nat told me that he had to "act bad in order to survive." He stole $12 from a used car lot and was also sent to the "Negro training school." Some months later he was transferred without any preparation from this training school to the desegregated Juvenile Evaluation Center. At this facility he began having dreams about white boys and African American boys sitting together in the center's dining room, watching the white and African American girls. In one dream he saw an African American girl, a white American girl, and himself. He told the African American girl that she had nice hair. Then the African American girl walked toward the white American girl and pointed to the white girl's hair and asked the patient what he thought about the white American's hair. Having such dreams made Nat anxious.

The third patient was a very handsome fourteen-year-old boy. He was the youngest of six siblings. As he was growing up, he perceived his father as the weak partner of the marriage. He was named by his mother and oldest brother after a very famous white movie star who was appearing in popular cowboy movies. The patient had no idea why this name was given to him. He was sensitive about his name. While he did not want to be associated with the famous "white cowboy" on a conscious level, his early memories and childhood daydreams were full of preoccupations with cowboys and with horses. Like Nat's family had done, this patient's family had also moved from a rural area to an urban area about two years before I saw him. This move caused him to notice more white persons in his new environment and to have more exposure to racism. The patient was sent to the African American training school because he had stolen food from a neighbor. From the training school, he was transferred to the Juvenile Evaluation Center and soon he was diagnosed as someone with schizophrenia. While talking with me he also verbalized sexual desire for both African American and white American girls at the center.

Clarence was twelve years old. His mother was never married to his father. They stayed together until Clarence was three months old; after two years his father died in an automobile accident. Clarence was raised by his maternal grandparents since his mother practically became an alcoholic and was in jail most of the time. About a year before I met him his mother was again sentenced to six months in jail. Clarence became very upset. The grandparents were not able to manage him, and, therefore, he was placed in a foster home. After running away from the foster home, Clarence was sent to the training school for African American male children, later to be transferred to the Juvenile Evaluation Center.

Before he went to the desegregated location, he had thought that white people were mean and, therefore, he took a flight to passivity and made a point of saying, "How do you do," to every white person he saw at the evaluation center. Once he was hit in the abdomen by a white boy. After this he developed gastrointestinal symptoms and had an "auditory hallucination" in which a man's voice would tell him that someone would die. While talking with me he recalled that his grandparents had told him to stay away from white people and white people's homes; otherwise he would be beaten up, punished, or lynched. Psychological testing at Cherry Hospital revealed no evidence of psychosis.

These four youngsters knew each other at the "Negro training school." Then they were among the first ten African American male "juvenile delinquents" who were sent to the desegregated center. Some weeks after I started to meet with them I noted that they had been involved in what later I would call a "therapeutic play" (Volkan, 2010) in order in order to stay "sane" under their difficult situation. During a psychoanalytic process, a "therapeutic play" is not described in words. It is expressed with activities that typically continue for days, weeks, or months and reflects a story of the patient's key mental conflict. The four youngsters wrote or cowrote poems. The fourteen-year-old youngster who was named after the famous "white cowboy" appeared to be their leader. With his permission these youngsters recited their poems to me.

Poem 1

Once there was a colored man from way up East
You can tell he was a pool shark from Hundred and Twenty Street
This white man wanted to shoot him a game
But the way the colored man was going to beat him was a crying
    shame
Colored man took the first shot and busted the balls
You can tell by the look in the white man's eyes he was going to lose
    them all
O! Colored man, hit the one, two and three
It was the prettiest shot you ever did see
He hit the four and pocketed the five
Hot water jumped from the white man's eyes

Took the sixth and seventh for a tough ride
Hit the eight and nine without touching the rails
Took the ten and eleven for the big wheel
White man said, "O Nigger, O Nigger, you don't beat me once, you
    don't beat me twice,
Fall down on your knees and shoot me some dice."
Colored man said "Your dice game is hard,
Introduce me to a deck and I will play you some cards."
White man spread ace, joker, king and queen
Colored man put a switch in the deck, the world had never seen
O Hobo*, over there sitting on the side,
Peeped over there and seeing the switch, croaked and died
White man reached back with tears in his eyes
And fell right down by the Hobo's side
Now the white man lies stiff as a door
The devil could not pay him to come back and gamble no more.

---

*the boys reported that the hobo was an African American

Poem 2

In 1943 I have seen the funniest fight you ever did see
This white man and colored man were fighting over a penny
The way the white man hit the colored man was a shame and a pity
The colored man staggered back and said, "You are death bound."
The white man got scared and started stamping the ground
He ran so fast that nothing could pass
But the colored man studied the cutting of his ass
He crawled on his stomach, he messed around and fell
The colored man said, "You better hold on the hell."
The devil said, "I don't want him tumbling down my pass
Because you cut all the skin off his ass."
The devil took and sent him to the Lord's way
The Lord told him to stand half-way
He was standing half-way, bleeding like a well
He said, "I wonder what the government will pay
If I have to do that every day.
Colored man must have been some kin to Jack Benny*
Because he sure killed me over a penny."

---

*Jack Benny was a famous white American comedian who pretended
to be very stingy.

Poem 3

Once there was a Jew from way up North
You can tell he was stingy the way he talked
He came to a rich man's house*, asking for a dime
He hoped God will kill him, that his baby was dying
The man said, "If you do not get out my place before I count nine
I am starting to cut your Jewish behind."
The Jew took three steps back like he had something in his mind
"I'd fight you man, but it ain't my dime."
The white man pulled a knife, started swinging
But the Jew broke and run, it was a crying shame
He ran, he tumbled and messed around and fell
From this day on he is groping in hell.

The rich man was associated with a white man

Poems 4 and 5

Unfortunately, I no longer have the full texts of poems 4 and 5. In poem 4 there is also reference to Jewish people in the USA. In this poem "once there was a colored man way down from South." He was known for performing fellatio, because of "the shape of his mouth." He went to a Jew's house. The Jew grabbed his gun and colored man "hit the floor" as dead.

The last poem that the youngsters had recited for me was written by Nat. In the poem a man whom Nat refers as "I" at some point of the poem, takes a promiscuous African American woman to an alley to have intercourse. There the man sees his father and brother who also want to have sexual relations with the woman. A policeman, who was associated with whiteness and authority, appears at the scene and orders the African American men to stop having intercourse. Then the African American woman invites the white policeman to join in the process.

The four youngsters made no free associations to the poems. All of them had come from low socioeconomic conditions with very difficult family problems. A theme openly expressed in their writings was of deadly fights between African Americans and white Americans. In the 1950s and early 1960s "the factor of segregation is interpreted as punishment for being black and necessarily makes the white ego-ideal a hostile one" (Kennedy, 1952, p. 314). I sensed that it was difficult to know who the winner was in some poems. In Poem 1 the white man loses the games to an African

American man; however, another African American, the hobo, dies before the white man dies. I also wondered if the youngsters' facing sudden desegregation and becoming preoccupied with white–black conflict also was being utilized as part of their psychological defense mechanism to conceal basic personality difficulties.

I was intrigued by their references to the American Jews. Did they externalize their minority status to another minority group who are white people in the United States? Perhaps the Jewish people stood for African Americans living in the North who, unlike the youngsters from the South, did not experience desegregation. I surmised that facing sudden desegregation inflamed the fight between the four teenagers' victim selves and the internalized oppressors.

Beginning my life in Charlottesville

The four African American teenagers made a great impression on me. They were discharged from Cherry Hospital within two months or so and were sent back to the desegregated Juvenile Evaluation Center. I have no more information about them. As I stated in the introduction to this book, I came to Charlottesville, Virginia in 1963 and began my journey as a faculty member at the University of Virginia. This was the year when my family in Cyprus had begun to live in an enclave surrounded by their enemies. I became an American citizen in 1968.

When I began working at the University of Virginia Hospital, I do not recall meeting a physician or a head nurse who was African American. I recall African Americans not eating in the same dining area where white American hospital employees had their meals. Unofficially at least, some type of segregation of color or position was still going on. I think it was in 1966 that for the first time an African American patient was admitted to University of Virginia Hospital's psychiatric inpatient service. He was a rather popular figure with connections to professional sports. Later the hospital authorities opened the psychiatric inpatient services only to selected African Americans covered by insurance or private payers until having African Americans as inpatients would become a routine activity.

In those days some rich white families in Charlottesville would host outings for psychiatric inpatients and the patients could use their swimming pools. After African Americans began to be admitted as psychiatric patients some of them refused to have African American patients visit their homes and use their swimming pools. The acceptance of societal transformation was not easy.

A couple of years later after becoming a faculty member at the University of Virginia I travelled hundreds and hundreds of times between Charlottesville and Washington, DC to undergo my personal psychoanalysis and study psychoanalysis at the Washington Psychoanalytic Institute. I became a psychoanalyst myself. I was also aware of my survivor guilt: my living safely in the United States while my parents, sisters, other family members, and friends in Cyprus were forced to stay under subhuman conditions. I am sure that my personal history at this time, combined with my earlier experiences at Cherry Hospital, made me notice more and more "oppressed" African Americans within my environment.

When I became the acting chairperson of the Department of Psychiatry at the University of Virginia in 1977, I broke the existing tradition of not inviting African Americans—most of them were attendants at the Department of Psychiatry—to the department's social events. In 1978 I was appointed to be the medical director of the Blue Ridge Hospital when this facility, formerly for individuals with tuberculosis, was given to the University of Virginia. Blue Ridge Hospital would be closed eighteen years later when the new University Hospital was built. As the medical director, I selected a female African American as the second administrator of the Blue Ridge Hospital. She, as I expected, turned out to be most effective in helping me to run a hospital. We developed a habit of having lunch in historical downtown at least once a month for many years. I was aware that I wanted to show the people in this crowded location how a white man and an African American lady can be friends and equal human beings.

It is beyond the aim of this book to explore the causes of slavery and racism in the United States and the many positive changes leading to more acceptance of human diversity within the country during the last few decades, including the election of an African American, Barack Obama, as the president of the United States. Yet, in the introduction to this book I described open expressions of racism and ethnocentrism in Charlottesville in August 2017 by white Americans who were not residents of my city.

Joseph Montville, a former diplomat who was a member of the Center for the Study of Mind and Human Interaction (CSMHI) organized and conducted three meetings in 2018 and 2019 at The Point of View International Retreat and Research Center, owned by George Mason University's School for Conflict Analysis and Resolution near Washington,

DC, to look at the American Civil War at 150 years and come up with ideas for healing deep wounds. Well-known figures from different Christian denominations and others with backgrounds in history, criminal justice, and conflict resolution came together. I was able to attend two of these meetings. As expected, discussing slavery and how it is remembered differently by African Americans and white Americans were the main topics. Some individuals' stories were very moving. When I heard about the lives of many young African Americans in a Virginia jail and how they are treated in 2019, once more I remembered my four patients who had written poems in 1962.

In the following chapters I will begin to explore present societal division in the United States and similar situations in other countries.

CHAPTER EIGHT

Who are we now?

In 1995 Europe was on the verge of an unprecedented era of social, economic, and political cooperation. Yet, there was a resurgence of racism and shared hostile and malignant prejudice in Western Europe. In Central and Eastern Europe, many fragments of the old Soviet Union had disintegrated into ethnic violence and genocidal warfare. That year I formed the Committee on Neo-Racism at the Center for the Study of Mind and Human Interaction (CSMHI). Four years earlier the European Parliament's Committee on Inquiry into Racism and Xenophobia had issued a Joint Declaration Against Racism and Xenophobia. In the Introduction to this report the reader could read the following statement: "Racism and xenophobia spring from the individual's fear and insecurity about the future and are nurtured by unemployment and poverty. The removal of these factors should be a prime policy aim for Europe's national and local authorities as well as the European Community." This statement reflected a conceptualization of racism and xenophobia in a simplistic way. My purpose for forming the CSMHI committee was to explore neo-racism, especially in Europe, from a psychological angle *in depth*. Members of the committee included psychoanalysts as well as scholars from other backgrounds, such as history, sociology, and diplomacy from the United States, Turkey, Israel, Finland, Germany, and Russia. Two psychoanalysts from the USA had come originally from Ghana and India. For two years we had meetings in Charlottesville as well as in Ankara, Turkey under the sponsorship of the Deputy Undersecretary of Foreign Affairs of the Republic of Turkey and the Ministry of Foreign Affairs' Center for Strategic Research.

According to some historians, the roots of hostile prejudice and persecution in Europe started as early as the tenth century, and certainly was evident throughout the Middle Ages. Jews, Cathars, lepers, witches, and others were perceived as inherently threatening and evil, and were persecuted in various ways. During the work of the CSMHI committee we noted how the collapse of the Soviet Union occasioned not only the removal of the old "enemy," but also a sudden increase in the number of immigrants fleeing political turmoil. This was in addition to those immigrants already arriving from "non-Christian" countries to the south and east and guest workers especially in Germany (Thomson, Harris, Volkan, & Edwards, 1995).

One of the participants of the CSMHI committee, the late Princeton University historian Norman Itzkowitz, referred to the situation in Europe during the late part of the twentieth century as the time for ethnic awakening. I began focusing on the metaphorical question, "Who are we now?" that emerges within a population following the breakup of a political system or drastic revolutionary change, whether we consider it "good" or "bad," a war or war-like situation. During the CSMHI's committee work we were noticing how the colonialists leaving Africa, the reunification of East Germany with West Germany in 1990, the collapse of the Soviet Union and the former Yugoslavia in 1991 had played a significant role in the development of the metaphorical question, "Who are we now?" in Europe.

My focus in this chapter is on the present-day spread of the same metaphorical question globally and the world entering into "Who Are We Now Civilization" (Volkan, 2018c, 2019). I will now describe what factors have created such a civilization and its observable symptoms which include societal division in many countries, the building of walls, and many individuals' search for a political leader who, they imagine, will focus on the protection of large-group identity and bringing back old glories.

Changes at an unprecedented pace and scale

Incredible advances in communication, signal and photographic intelligence and travel technologies, and expanded financial markets beyond national borders in the twenty-first century, have made people with different large-group identities interact to a greater degree and with greater speed. When I was a child, China in my mind was an unreachable place and I could construct life there only according to my fantasies. Now I see

Chinese people almost everywhere I travel. Last year I gave a dozen seminars on psychoanalytic topics to hundreds of Chinese students while sitting in my home in Virginia, pushing a button on my computer. As I was writing this book in North Cyprus, I attended a graduation ceremony at a medical school in Nicosia. Two graduating students were introduced as the most successful ones in their class. They were from Nigeria. A Cypriot Turkish friend of mine moved to a new house near a beach on the island to settle with his wife as a newly retired person. He noticed that all the houses surrounding his new house are occupied by Russians. Hundreds of Russians now own houses or apartments in North Cyprus. My friend wanted to greet his neighbors while they were passing by his house. But the Russians ignored him. He was shocked. If his neighbors were other Cypriot Turks his relationship with them would be very different. This is a simple example that illustrates the appearance of prejudices as well as jealousies when we notice different customs linked to large-group identity issues.

Historian and psychoanalyst Peter Loewenberg (1995) wrote about people from different cultures and religions coming together and creating "synthetic nations," such as the United States, Israel, and Brazil. In our present world, the idea of having an ethnically pure national identity, or of being a "synthetic nation" but composed of *only* selected people from *selected* locations, is an illusion.

During the last few decades, a modern form of "globalization" has become the buzzword in political as well as academic circles. It personifies an idea and attempts to promote prosperity and well-being for societies by standardizing economic, technological, ecological, and sociocultural elements and by bringing political democratic freedom to every part of the world. From a psychological point of view this wished-for form of internationalism implies erasing "Otherness" to a great extent, which is an impossible task. Meanwhile younger generations, with their preoccupation with available communication technology, have begun to change the culture of older generations worldwide without being aware of what they are doing (Arnett, 2002; Twemlow & Sacco, 2008). Thus, the advantages that modern globalization provide are accompanied by some losses pertaining to traditional aspects of various cultures. What is most significant to note is the fact that the aggressive aspect of human nature and the killing of Others in the name of large-group identity remains the same. The best that technology in the twenty-first century offers mostly is in the service of protecting large-group identities by increasing the military capability to destroy Others.

Genetic research

Various types of genealogical DNA tests have become popular worldwide, sometimes confusing people about their ancestors. When I was a youngster, I was taught that my Turkish ancestors had come from Central Asia. Modern research tells us that we all have a common birthplace somewhere in Africa and because of this we share most of our genetic information (Cann, Stoneking, & Wilson, 1987; Yu, Fu, & Li, 2002). There is information illustrating how Cypriot Turks and Cypriot Greeks share very similar DNA results (Baysal et al., 1992). I became aware how some people on the island did not want to hear this fact and experienced large-group identity confusion.

During the American Sociological Association's 112th annual meeting in Montreal in August 2017, Aaron Panofsky, from the Institute for Society and Genetics, University of California, Los Angeles presented his and his colleagues' findings illustrating mixed ancestry among white supremacists. Following this the news media explored how white supremacists held on to a denial mechanism and accused the researchers of being Jewish conspirators.

On the eve of the Second International Summit on Human Genome Editing on November 27–28, 2018 in Hong Kong, a Chinese researcher named He Jiankui, who had had some of his training in the USA, shocked the world by claiming to have altered the genomes of fraternal twin baby girls in mid-October. The girls' genomes have been permanently altered, so the modification will be passed on if the girls have children. The alteration was intended to make the girls' cells resistant to HIV infection. However, some genes escaped from modification. So, the girls still can get HIV. He Jiankui's irresponsible behavior violated the ethical consensus of scientists all over the world. We can imagine that, in the future, there will be more human genome editing under ethical conditions. We can wonder how such development will create large-group identity confusion.

Robots

In July 2018, Tufts University in Boston, Massachusetts, announced the United States' first graduate-degree program in human–robot interaction. Tufts University wished to provide students with opportunities and resources for intellectual and personal growth through transformational experiences inside and outside the classroom and also meet the needs of society.

I became very interested in this development after one of my teenage grand-daughters sent me a video. She had gone to a museum in Washington, DC. The video showed her dancing with a robot at the museum. I recalled my joking about Martians coming to Earth and forcing human beings from different races or ethnic backgrounds to come together against a common enemy. Soon we will be "invaded" by robots. This will make an impact on large-group identity issues.

The human mind cannot keep pace with the incredible changes that result from advanced technology. Furthermore, such developments, alongside their positive aspects, have led to cyber attacks, have created conflicts among large groups, and have brought confusion and confrontation to large-group identities. There is extreme interest in and necessary funding for what the human mind can develop technologically, but there is less interest—sometimes no interest—in funds to study the human mind's adjustment to accelerating changes in the environment.

Refugees, immigrants, and international terrorism

Early in the twenty-first century the negative aspects of modern globalization and its connection with terrorism were noted by different scholars (for example see: Çevik, 2003; Kinnvall, 2004; Stapley, 2006) before we witnessed the horrors of Al-Qaeda and ISIS. Two books I published in 2017, one with Finnish historian Jouni Suistola, are on refugees and terrorism (Suistola & Volkan, 2017; Volkan, 2017b). In this book I will not dwell on the psychology of refugees, forced or voluntary immigrants, and my work with newcomers in several countries. Also I will not present the history of terrorism and will not describe highjacking religion for terrorism and the present-day terroristic activities.

Europe is facing a "refugee crisis." But a similar situation exists in many other places. For example, Kenya has been known as the home of the largest refugee camp in the world on the Kenya–Somalia border. Most refugees there come from Somalia, which has been torn by civil war. Cambodia is filled with refugees from the Khmer Rouge; in fact, the whole country is a refugee from the years of slaughter. Over two and a half million persons in Turkey who escaped from Syria have created huge practical, as well as political and cultural problems for that country. In my previous work I noted that, accompanying societal reactions to many traumas, medical problems, legal, political, financial, and other practical issues and security concerns, there is always an increased investment in large-group identity by both refugees and persons in the host countries.

Terrorist attacks—April 2013 in Boston, November 2015 in Paris, December 2015 in San Bernardino, March 2016 in Brussels, July 2016 in Nice, and December 2016 in Berlin—and other similar events since then have linked terrorism not only with lone-wolf newcomers, but also with refugees in general in the Western world. It should be remembered that terrorist incidents, in greater numbers than those that took place in the Western world, have occurred in other locations of the globe: in Ankara, Baghdad, Benghazi, Kabul, Madagali, Kabul, and dozens and dozens of other places. Tragedies created by Al-Qaeda and ISIS have illustrated large-group identity separation between Muslims and Christians. Such separations have also occurred between other religions. The Rohingya people, a stateless Indo-Aryan ethnic group, the majority of whom are Muslim while a minority are Hindu, were forced to leave Myanmar and enter Bangladesh. We became aware of hatred and religious intolerance by ultra-nationalist Buddhists. We also see worldwide purification activities through the erasing of symbols of other religions—the destruction of churches, synagogues, or mosques, for example—in order to "stabilize" a large group's identity.

Many persons in the host countries perceive refugees as the Other and experience benign, hostile, or malignant prejudice against the newcomers. Psychologically speaking, the main fear is the contamination of their large-group identity by the identity of the Other. We can easily imagine that those who are able to keep their individual identities from the impact of large-group sentiments become more willing to open up the metaphorical large-group tent and accept the huge number of newcomers. Those who perceive the newcomers as tearing holes in, and thus damaging, the metaphorical tent's canvas—the border of large-group identity—become anxious and defensively perceive the huge immigrant population as a major threat.

For a deeper understanding of severe societal/political divisions within a country we need to consider the idea of turning a political party or a political/ideological organization—such as the Ku Klux Klan or other white supremacy movements in the United States, or PEDIGA (European Patriots against the Islamization of the Occident) in Germany—into the second type of large-group identity that develops in adulthood as I described in Chapter Three or at least making it resemble this type of large-group identity.

Basic trust and blind trust

Eric Erikson (1985) used the term "basic trust" to describe how a child learns to feel comfortable putting his or her own safety in a caretaker's hands. By developing basic trust, a child discovers, in turn, how to trust him- or herself. In normal circumstances, adults who depend on trusting themselves and others can see the beauty of diversities in human beings without anxiety.

Antonius Robben (2000) provided a good example on the assault on basic trust when he studied families in Argentina after the country's "Dirty War" that raged from 1976 to 1983. The next year Slavica Jurcevic and Ivan Urlic (2001) published similar findings when they carried out a study with families of disappeared sons from the 1991–1995 war in Croatia. I examined Albania and Romania after dictators Enver Hoxha and Nicolae Ceauşescu, respectively, were gone (Volkan, 1997, 2004) and described how basic trust was lost in these countries. For example, during these times, an Albanian mother could be sent to exile if her child, while attending school, spoke about her mother's complaint of the quality of bread she had bought that morning. People spying for Enver Hoxha were present at schools listening to students' remarks about their adult family members. Parents could not "trust" their own children. Under such societal conditions, in order to escape fear and anxiety, many people in Albania and Romania developed "blind trust" in the dictators.

Enver Hoxha and Nicolae Ceauşescu created a new large-group identity for their followers during their adulthood, interfered with democratic processes and human rights issues, and caused severe division within the total population. I learned that even though there were no mass suicides or mass killings Albanian and Romanian families were divided into "good" and "bad" categories, people were exiled from their homes, and dissenters were tortured or even killed.

Conservatism and liberalism

Political conservatism consciously or unconsciously intensifies large-group identity markers to societal, religious, economic, and educational practices with an aim to bring back or keep an old glory and to increase the members' shared self-esteem. Before proceeding further, I must state that conservatism is not a "bad" word. It exists all over the world. The nature of conservatism changes, however, when many individuals in a society perceive threats against their large-group identity, with or without being aware of this condition, while the authoritarian conservative leader, in order to stay in power, increases the sense of expected shared victimhood and unfairness through political propaganda (Prince, 2018; Volkan, 2014a). Such a development increases paranoid expectations and hostile prejudice against the Other, including people in the same country who are not followers of the authoritarian leader.

At the present time "Who are we now civilization" has shaken many individuals' basic trust in different parts of the world, replacing it with "blind trust" in a transforming political leader who is conservative and authoritarian and who attempts to turn a political party or organization into a second-type large-group identity for his or her followers. We see an increase in right-wing political parties in many locations. They have emerged also in Europe, such as FIDEZS (Fidezs-Hungarian Civic Alliance) and Jobbik (Movement for a Better Hungary) in Hungary, UKIP (UK Independence Party) in Britain, AfD (Alternative für Deutschland) in Germany, SD (Swedendemocrats) in Sweden, PS (Finns Party) in Finland, PiS (Law and Justice Party) in Poland, RN (Rassemblement National) in France, FPÖ (Freedom Party) in Austria, PVV (Party for Freedom) in the Netherlands, and SRS (Serbian Radical Party) in Serbia. I have not closely studied the impact of the leaders of these political parties on their societies. As I was writing this book, Boris Johnson, the pro-Brexit politician, was chosen as the leader of the ruling Conservative party and became prime minister in the UK. He, like Donald Trump, promised to restore to his country the glory of the past.

Some authoritarian leaders who pretend to behave in a democratic fashion, and stay away from torturing and killing opponents, may perform "soul murders." Leonard Shengold (1991) originally used the term "soul murder" to refer to the abuse or neglect of children that deprives them of their identity and ability to experience joy in life. Here I use his term to illustrate how an authoritarian political leader/regime fills many citizens' lives with helplessness and fear, and interferes with or even ruins their enjoyment of daily activities. Their ability to assert themselves may be very difficult or even lost. Many liberal minded people in the present-day Turkey are experiencing "soul murder" (Suistola & Volkan, 2017).

Since I mentioned conservatism, I will also say a few words about liberalism. Broadly speaking, liberalism supports individual autonomy, civil rights, racial and gender equality, secularism, and freedom of speech.

Shared political liberalism may induce societal difficulties if it becomes a force against the "normal" sense of large-group identity and "benign" prejudice which, as I examined earlier, everyone develops in childhood and which does not humiliate any human being.

Building walls

Deniz Arıboğan (2018), a member of the International Dialogue Initiative (IDI), informed us about the significant increase in the number of physical walls and fences around the world. For example, Hungary built barricades against immigrants, and Austria decided to create a fence along the Slovenian border. New walls arose between Pakistan and Bangladesh, between the United Arab Emirates and Oman, between Botswana and Zimbabwe, and between Malaysia's Limbang district and Brunei. Arıboğan stated that the new walls and fences erected all over the world are different from border fortifications of the past. In today's world they are built for redefining identities and societal–political aims.

During his presidential campaign Donald Trump referred to himself as "Mr. Brexit." Brexit can be understood as allowing only a selected type of people to settle in England. Donald Trump presented his role as being a purifier of the United States identity from unwanted Others. He read "Snake," which was written by a soul singer and radical African American activist, Oscar Brown, Jr., in 1963 and was released as a song by singer Al Wilson in 1968. Snake tells the story of a tenderhearted woman who saw a half-frozen snake, wrapped it in silk cloth, and hurried home. She took good care of the snake and saved its life. But later when she kissed the snake and held it tight the snake gave her a vicious bite. Oscar Brown's daughters became furious with Donald Trump when the president used the poem for his own propaganda and insulted Oscar Brown's deep respect for humanity.

Donald Trump's focus on building a wall at the US–Mexican border, his promise to keep people from certain countries from entering the United States, and declaring "America First," were significant elements to his being elected the 45th president of the United States (Volkan, 2018b, 2019).

The political leader's personality

The personality characteristics of a political leader can initiate and/or become intertwined with societal and political processes and inflame or tame populations' responses to the metaphorical question "Who are we now?" The term "personality" describes the observable and predictable repetitions that an individual consciously and unconsciously utilizes under ordinary circumstances to "maintain a stable reciprocal relationship between the individual and his or her environment. Therefore, personality is associated with self-regulatory and environment-altering ego functions that an individual uses regularly to maintain both internal (intrapsychic) and interpersonal harmony" (Volkan, Akhtar, Dorn, Kafka, Kernberg, Olsson, Rogers, & Shanfield, 1998, p. 152). Two additional concepts, *temperament* and *character*, are usually included under the umbrella of personality. Temperament refers to genetically and constitutionally determined affectomotor tendencies. Character is formed by the modes an individual utilizes to reconcile intrapsychic conflicts during developmental years. When temperament and character are combined, they produce adult personality.

The concept of personality is not the same as identity—the latter is not observed by others, but instead is sensed only by a specific individual. Identity refers to an individual's inner sense of sameness, a continuity of personalized past, present, and future, and stable body and gender images (Akhtar, 1992). The term "personality" should also be differentiated from "self-representation"—a common psychoanalytic term that refers to a psychoanalyst's metapsychological description of how his or her patient's self-organization (or personality organization) has developed and how it theoretically relates to self and object images as well as id demands, ego functions, and superego influences.

In our clinical work we observe various types of personalities and name them obsessive, narcissistic, depressive, and so on. For example, when we see a patient who is habitually dogmatic, opinionated, ambivalent, and "clean," and exhibits stiff and rigid gestures and cannot freely express emotions, we say that this patient has an obsessive personality.

The personalities of our political leaders, in a general sense but not necessarily a psychoanalytic sense, have always been scrutinized, especially during elections, crises, or scandals. Over the course of an adult individual's lifetime, he or she exhibits habitual behavior and thought patterns, emotional expressions, modes of speech, and bodily gestures which can be observed by others. Because political leaders spend a great deal of time in the public eye, and have little choice but to allow much of their life and personal habitual patterns to be available to everyone through the media, attempts are sometimes made to analyze their personality.

In 1993 I joined a group of psychiatrists and we formed a team to study some political leaders' personality characteristics and psychodynamics of their decision-making processes. We met twice a year for five years and published our findings (Volkan, Akhtar, Dorn, Kafka, Kernberg, Olsson, Rogers, & Shanfield, 1998). We noted that a leader with obsessional personality organization typically tries to find a solution by searching for some rule, principle, or external requirement to supply the "right answer." Such a leader may over-value bureaucracy and promote too many decisions on the basis of rules and regulations, reducing needed creativity, autonomy, and political diversity, especially during times of crisis. We noted that a leader may, of course, have "normal" obsessional traits or have definite obsessional personality problems. As an example of a leader who demonstrated the adaptive qualities of a well-functioning obsessional style, we referred to President Woodrow Wilson. Wilson had the scholarly capacity to research, organize, and communicate his ideas. He demanded perfection of himself in his writing style. His speeches are considered among the best of American presidents. But, we noted, his obsessional personality also caused problems. We mentioned Menachem Begin of Israel as another political leader with obsessional personality.

We also studied political leaders with paranoid personality and concluded:

> Modest degrees of paranoid thinking combined with self-righteousness and a socially directed cause can combine into politically adaptive technique. These leaders have the ability to arouse within the followers an identification with the leader and the goals espoused, and a means of accomplishing these ends. The presence of a paranoid trait, therefore, does not always imply abnormality. (Volkan, Akhtar, Dorn, Kafka, Kernberg, Olsson, Rogers, & Shanfield, 1998, p 155)

We read distinguished political theoretician Robert Tucker's excellent biography of Joseph Stalin. Tucker reported that Stalin allegedly told a colleague, "The greatest delight is to mark one's enemy, prepare everything, avenge oneself thoroughly and then go to sleep" (1973, p. 211). Later I had a chance to interview Stalin's two private interpreters, Valentin Berezhkov and Zoya Zarubina (Volkan, 1991b, 2013). They told me stories about Stalin's private life including burning people with his cigarette when he did not like their comments. Definitely Stalin was a destructive, paranoid, and malignant transforming leader.

We also wondered about leaders with schizoid personality. We studied observable behavioral patterns of Otto von Bismarck, the Prussian statesman who was a dominant figure in Europe from the 1860s to 1890, and concluded that he might have schizoid personality. Spiritual and mystical matters often have great appeal for such leaders. They fluctuate between nimble eloquence and clumsy inarticulateness.

> Beneath their detachment lies an exquisite sensitive and emotionally needy self. The possession of such a self, while often expressed through a preference for solitary occupations and discomfort in group endeavors, can also propel such individuals toward leadership roles—as if through leadership they can meet the needs of their dependency. (Volkan, Akhtar, Dorn, Kafka, Kernberg, Olsson, Rogers, & Shanfield, 1998, p. 156)

America's fixation with Donald Trump's personality

In the United States many scholars, including some psychiatrists, and people from the news media have publicly stated that Donald Trump has a narcissistic personality. They have described how he is always busy presenting himself as "number one" and "greatest" while he compulsively insults and humiliates his opponents. He wants America, like himself, to be "great" and protected by a "border." Michael D'Antonio's (2016) biography of Donald Trump also describes his subject's endless demands for great achievements while lacking the ability to have empathy for those who are his opponents or people around him.

In the introduction to this book I wrote how Donald Trump found "very fine people" as well as "hatred, bigotry, and violence" within protestors with Nazi flags as well as counterprotestors in Charlottesville. He has been inflaming the "Who are we now?" question in front of the American population and playing a crucial role in maintaining a societal/political division in the United States.

Preponderance of gun violence in the United States is well known (Volkan, 2016). As I was writing this book, the 250th mass shooting in 2019 took place on August 3 in El Paso, Texas. It was a hate crime. Psychological factors in a person's own internal world play a role in his or her becoming a shooter. A president of a country is a transference figure. Many wondered if the gunman at El Paso had been influenced by Donald Trump's rhetoric about the Latino invasion.

I had offers to write Donald Trump's psychobiography. I declined to do so. It took my coauthor historian Norman Itzkowitz and me seven years to write a psychobiography of Kemal Atatürk, the founder of modern Turkey (Volkan & Itzkowitz, 1984). He and I, and also Andrew Dod, worked for three years to complete Richard Nixon's biography (Volkan, Itzkowitz, & Dod, 1997). We were able to interview many individuals who knew our subjects when they were alive. We examined information from our subjects' childhood, early traumas, growth-inducing experiences, and crystallization of their personality organizations during the adolescence passage. Our subjects' entire lives were looked at developmentally through a psychoanalytic lens. I take writing the psychobiography of someone who was not on my couch as a serious and difficult challenge. I have no preparation for examining Donald Trump's life.

Since there is so much interest in Donald Trump's personality in the United States and in leaders with exaggerated narcissism in other places, in the next chapter I will present my colleagues' and my clinical findings on narcissistic personality and illustrate the various types of behavior patterns individuals with this personality typically exhibit.

CHAPTER NINE

Persons with exaggerated narcissism

Narcissism refers to love of self and is linked to self-preservation. In human psychological functioning, it is as normal as sex, aggression, and anxiety (Rangell, 1980; Volkan & Ast, 1994; Weigert, 1967). Like sex, aggression, and anxiety it is subject to variation. It can be "healthy" or "unhealthy" according to the individual's own perception as well as to the judgment of the clinician who investigates the individual's inner world. Many factors can interfere with the development of healthy narcissism, and some people develop exaggerated narcissism, while others hold on to depleted narcissism to some degree or another.

In the 1960s and 1970s, there was a concentrated effort in American psychoanalytic circles to study patients with exaggerated narcissism. Heinz Kohut (1966, 1971, 1977) posited an independent line of development from autoerotism through narcissism to a higher form of narcissism that is adaptive and culturally valuable. Maternal shortcomings lead to a fixation in the child at a level short of the higher-level narcissism, and the child develops a grandiose and exhibitionistic self-image that Kohut called the *grandiose self*. If the maternal shortcomings have not been too great, the grandiose self is transformed into a self with mature ambitions and self-esteem.

While Kohut was developing his metapsychological understanding of narcissism, following Edith Jacobson (1964), Otto Kernberg (1975, 1976, 1980) described individuals who have narcissistic personality and who utilize splitting of self and object images as their main defense mechanism. Kernberg also used the term "grandiose self" in describing the omnipotent part of the self that such patients exhibit overtly.

Kernberg's grandiose self is formed from the fusion of three elements: the real self, the ideal self, and the ideal object. The *real self* is the specialness of the child reinforced by early experiences with mother and other important persons with mothering functions in the child's environment. The *ideal self* is the self-image that is endowed with power, beauty, or wealth to compensate the child's normative frustration in his or her environment; the ideal self-image also helps the child manage disconcerting and difficult early emotions such as rage and envy. The *ideal object* is the fantasized image of the limitlessly providing mother figure.

At the same time, the "hungry" (for psychological nurturing) part of the child's self-representation, fused with unacceptable aspects of the real self and with devalued object images, is separated from the grandiose self through splitting. In the typical person with narcissistic personality, the part with exaggerated narcissism is overt while the "hungry" part exists in a covert fashion. Throughout the developmental years, individuals make unconscious attempts to deny or externalize the hungry part of their developing personality, as such aspects of the self are markers of a vulnerably dependent, angry, envious, and/or disappointed self-experience.

It is beyond the scope of this book to describe and compare Kohut's and Kernberg's theoretical positions. The liveliness of the debates between Kohut's followers and those applying Kernberg's findings came to the attention of the psychiatric profession at large. In 1979 the *Diagnostic and Statistical Manual of the American Psychiatric Association* (APA) officially recognized Narcissistic Personality Disorder, described as a sense of self-importance, or uniqueness; preoccupation with fantasies of unlimited success; exhibitionistic need for constant attention and admiration; characteristic responses to threats of self-esteem; and characteristic disturbances in interpersonal relationships, such as feelings of entitlement, interpersonal explosiveness, relationships that alternate between the extremes of over-idealization and devaluation, and lack of empathy. The APA manual described persons with exaggerated narcissism.

In view of the fact that there are variations of problems with exaggerated narcissism, we should allow some flexibility in evaluating what is called pathological and what is not pathological. German psychoanalyst Gabriele Ast and I (Volkan & Ast, 1994) noted that narcissistic personality exists on a spectrum and ranges from being "successful" to being "malignant." Successful ones achieve a position in life where their inner sense of exaggerated self-love, being "number one" and above others, is actually verified by hundreds, thousands, or millions of people when they become adored popular icons, leaders of organizations, or influential political figures. Such individuals who possess intelligence, unconscious fantasies of being "saviors," and are capable of some sublimations are successful in achieving and maintaining a "fit" between their psychological wish and need for adoration, entitlement, and greatness and the responses they receive from the external world. On the other end of the spectrum, there are persons who are impelled to experience repeated aggressive triumphs over others who represent the "hungry" aspects of their self-representations and threatening devalued object images, in order to feel unique, strong, entitled, and defensively omnipotent. Their narcissism is contaminated with paranoid expectations. These are destructive narcissistic personalities. Individuals with either "successful" or "destructive" narcissistic personality organization do not think about seeking psychoanalytic treatment. When an external event threatens their narcissism, they may experience confusion and depression. Then they may consider arranging to see a psychoanalyst.

In the previous chapter I described my working with a team of psychiatrists starting in 1993 and examining political leaders with various types of personalities, including those with narcissistic personality. Earlier, between 1975 and 1981, I met weekly with a group of younger colleagues to discuss cases, including those with exaggerated narcissism. None of our patients with exaggerated narcissism were politicians. We called ourselves the Charlottesville Psychoanalytic Study Group. For years, we made formulations about the family background of patients who later develop exaggerated narcissism.

The mother's coldness and fantasies of omnipotence

As an infant and child, an individual who later will have narcissistic personality is left emotionally hungry by a cold mother, but is less traumatized by this experience than another similarly deprived infant/child that subsequently develops borderline or even psychotic personality. We agreed with Arnold Modell (1975) that the mental trauma inflicted when the child is building his or her sense of identity may lead to the establishment of a precocious and vulnerable sense of autonomy supported by fantasies of omnipotence. Personal identity problems and problems in the distribution of narcissism are always related. We expect to find problems with the distribution of love of self as well as love of others (objects) when the identity is not cohesive. Such children, as described by Modell, may also have had to defend themselves against excessive maternal intrusiveness.

Although the mother of such a patient was cold and ungiving, she saw the child as someone "special," perhaps more beautiful than other siblings, a savior of the family name, or an instrument for obtaining the mother's own narcissistic ends. The mother's own or the family's circumstances at the time of the child's birth played a role in inducing in the mother (and/or other mothering person) feelings that the newborn is "special." For example, one mother enduring complicated mourning viewed her young child as a link to dead siblings; the child was perceived as immortal and omnipotent. Although her complicated mourning process made her cold as a mother, she engaged in an intense relationship with the child, a relationship defined by an intense pressure on the child to attend and respond to her own psychological needs. In another situation, a Catholic mother prone to depression, in search of an idealized father of her own, viewed her son as special and had daydreams of his growing up to be the pope (idealized father). Her perception of her child as unique was deposited into the developing identity of the infant through the mother–child interaction and, to use Otto Kernberg's (1975, 1976) term, such interactions provided him with a special "real self." It is in such a core that the idealized self and idealized object images of the grandiose self are subsequently included, whereas the devalued self and other devalued object images that reflect the interaction with the cold mother are split off. Therefore, the behavior of the individual as an adult reflects a grandiose self beneath which can be found the separated aspect of the "hungry" infant.

When such a child comes to the oedipal age and maintains a rather omnipotent self-representation on the one hand and a "hungry" self-representation on the other, the child colors his or her oedipal self-images, as well as the oedipal parental images, with defensive splitting. This prevents the child from developing a cohesive superego. If the father is or is perceived as someone "dangerous" the child's fears of humiliation may become intertwined with castration fantasies. However, pre-oedipal issues are primarily responsible for a child to have a narcissistic personality as an adult.

Multiple mothers

There is another factor in the family environment that may prepare a foundation for the development of narcissistic (or borderline) personality organization. I am referring to a child's experience with "multiple mothers" during the developmental years. When I began practicing psychoanalysis in Charlottesville, I noted that some wealthy white families in the United States still kept the traditions of the Old South and raised their children with both the biological white mother and an African American nanny. In some families the white mothers, due to their own psychological/cultural motivations, would treat the African American nannies as second-class human beings. The nannies would take care and love the white children only in the basement, the kitchen, or outdoors. These children literally would have two separate "mothers" and escape much of the struggle involved in facing both good and bad aspects of one mother and integrating her opposing images. It was hard for them to unite opposite sides of one object's representation because they experienced early that when frustrated by one mothering figure, they could seek gratification from the other, all the while hiding the experience with one mother from the experience with the other one. Corresponding self-representations were also hard to mend and they had a possibility of developing narcissistic or borderline personality organization. Additionally, in order to adjust to the predominantly white environment in which they grew up, under certain circumstances such white children had to deny extremely good experiences with the African American "mother." They exaggerated narcissistic investment in the image of the white mother. In turn they felt themselves to be special children. I published the cases of two individuals with white and African American "mothers" (Volkan, 2010; Volkan & Fowler, 2009).

In some cultures, such as those found in Turkey or Arab countries in the Middle East where extended or modified extended families are routine, the child escapes the development of narcissistic or borderline personalities because the culture usually helps them to put multiple mothers/ caretakers in the extended or modified extended families on an emotional continuum. If the "multiple mothers" fight with one another and psychologically feel apart from each other, even if they come from the same social or racial background, this situation again taxes the integrative functions of the child's ego.

Revisiting replacement children

We also noted yet another phenomenon that may interfere with mending of opposing self- and object images. A mother who has a rather well-formed and idealized mental representation of a dead child or a dead relative may put this mental representation into the living child, thus making a part of the child's self-representation an unintegrated special container. I would like to add that not all replacement children develop psychopathology. When these children can integrate what was deposited in them, they have a strong sense of *generational continuity* and a strong sense of belonging to family and culture. Consecutively, this may increase self-confidence in a healthy way. Some replacement children, when they assimilate deposited images that had been highly idealized by the depositors, may in fact become adults with very healthy missions in life.

Need to be "number one"

Since a person with narcissistic personality psychologically needs to be "number one," it is no wonder that some of them seek political leadership. An examination of Richard Nixon's adult life reveals that the dominant aspect of his personality was narcissistic, although he utilized obsessional preoccupations to support his narcissism (Volkan, Itzkowitz, & Dod, 1997). Richard Nixon was a collector of "firsts." According to his wife, since the time they met in college, Nixon had always been "president of some group like the 20–30 Club, and this, that and the other thing" (Mazo & Hess, 1967, p. 30). He ran for thirteen elections, starting with class president in high school, and lost only three. At the age of thirty-three he was elected to the US Congress, became a US senator at the age of thirty-seven, and became the second youngest US vice president at the age of thirty-nine. As president, he continued to collect "firsts." Some were significant, such as recognition for normalizing relations with China. Some of them were trivial. For example, at the dedication of his library, he insisted that it was the *first* occasion honored by the presence of four First Ladies. According to his aide John Ehrlichman, "There was a running gag on any campaign; everything that happened was a 'historic first'" (Volkan, Itzkowitz, & Dod, 1997, p. 94).

A narcissistic leader's grandiosity masks a covertly fragile self-esteem. Anything that threatens such a leader's grandiosity or collections of "firsts" triggers shame, which may lead to unusual decisions to counteract it (Akhtar, 1992; Kernberg, 1975, 1976; Volkan & Ast, 1994).

The grandiose self in a glass bubble

Arnold Modell (1975) referred to *cocoon fantasies* among persons with narcissistic personality. In such fantasies, patients live alone in "cocoons." In my practice, I noted that typical patients with narcissistic personality have fantasies of living in a *glass bubble* (Volkan, 1979b, 2010). I suggest that the analogy of a glass bubble is more useful because it describes a transparent enclosure that permits its occupant to assess the world outside without being encroached upon and thus it enhances the patient's sense of omnipotence and self-sufficiency. Patients with narcissistic personality, while absorbed in self-interest, do have *intense* relationships with others; they watch people through the glass, in a sense, to see if others are going to adore or devalue them. Such patients will react to others according to their conscious and unconscious assessments of them, and they want to know if there are dangerous objects out there that may disturb their lonely kingdoms. The most dangerous object is the one that is degraded but which, through internalization, may contaminate the grandiose self. The glass bubble is in the service of maintaining an effective splitting.

Keeping themselves—in actuality, keeping their grandiose selves—"under glass" also indicates the kinds of interpersonal relations seen in typical cases. A cold and impervious material like glass represents their lack of warmth when interacting with others. This, in turn, reflects the probability of their having had a cold mother. Other meanings too, both conscious and unconscious, are usually condensed in the glass bubble fantasy. One typical meaning refers to the patient's unconscious wish to be the only child of the mother and receive all of her love. At the deepest level, the glass bubble represents the fantasy of mother's womb in which the idealized representation of the patient resides and forbids entry to any other siblings.

One of my patients literally referred to herself as a beautiful flower under glass (Volkan, 2010). But the "glass bubble" often appears in symbolic ways, such as in the case of an individual who repeatedly fantasized himself as being Robinson Crusoe *without* his Man Friday. There was no need to have Friday around because the patient believed himself omnipotent; the sea surrounding the Island of Juan Fernandez functioned as a "glass bubble."

The following is an example of an analysand in his early forties who actualized a glass bubble fantasy. During his analysis, when treatment began affecting his grandiose self, he became anxious. At this point, he came upon an article about a "one-man submarine" at Disney World in Florida that a customer could rent, submerge, and use to watch the underwater surroundings through glass. This patient had to fly to Florida to rent a one-man submarine, submerge it, and look at the fish and other things in the sea through the glass in order to bolster his self-sufficiency and his illusion that he needed no one. He later repeated this trip.

Individuals with narcissistic personality sometimes actualize their glass bubble fantasies on their psychoanalyst's couch so that during the sessions it may feel like the psychoanalyst's words hit a shield and do not enter the patient's mind. The analyst needs to tolerate this until the patient lowers the shield.

Next I want to illustrate the creation of a "glass bubble" in a historical arena.

Creating a "glass bubble" around Adolf Hitler

There have been many attempts to understand the mind of the man who presided over the Holocaust, and scholars have reviewed the various possible psychological influences on the formation of Hitler's personality (Volkan, Ast, & Greer, 2002). Since so much is known about Hitler and the Third Reich, I will not attempt to present a brief psycho-biography of Hitler. I will simply refer to the personality patterns that are reflected in his writings, such as *Mein Kampf* (1927). What we do know is that his ideology, propaganda, and activities aimed to create two collectives: the first, the Nazis, who were supposed to be tough, grandiose, superior, and powerful; the second, Jews, Roma people, and others deemed sub- or even nonhuman. The idea that the latter group had to be destroyed alone leads to the conclusion that Hitler's personality fits well with our understanding of the internal organization of malignant narcissism.

Hitler had an especially talented confederate in Joseph Goebbels, whom he appointed head of Nazi propaganda in 1928, and who is credited with creating the "Führer myth" while he was minister of propaganda and public enlightenment (*Propaganda und Volksaufklärung*) under the Third Reich. Austrian historian Victor Reimann—who was arrested by the Nazis in 1940 and spent the next five years in Nazi prisons—observed, "The Hitler/Goebbels combination is perhaps unique in world history" (1976, p. 2). Goebbels forbade jokes about the Führer and sought to conceal Hitler's personal weaknesses: Hitler's drawings and watercolors from his days as a struggling artist were collected so that no one could critique Hitler as an artist. Goebbels banned even the use of quotations from Hitler's *Mein Kampf* without the permission of his propaganda ministry. He made compulsory the use of the title "Führer" and introduced the greeting "Heil Hitler."

Goebbels was the architect of the "glass bubble" in which Hitler could maintain and hide his grandiose self where it could remain uncontaminated and unconnected with Nazi cruelties, so that any atrocities that came to light could be blamed on others. "If only the Führer knew became a byword in the Third Reich" (Reimann, 1976, p. 6). Hitler's image as a beneficent god in his "glass bubble" was presented to the post-1919 Treaty of Versailles Germans, who had been humiliated, both materially and emotionally.

Psychoanalyst Water Langer (1972) reported German press notices "to the effect that, 'As [Hitler] spoke, one heard God's mantle rustle through the room'; one German church group even passed a resolution stating that 'Hitler's word is God's law, the decrees and laws which represent it possess divine authority'" (Langer, 1972, p. 64). The party adopted a creed that clearly echoed Christian professions of faith: "We all believe, on this earth, in Adolf Hitler, our Führer, and we acknowledge that National Socialism is the only faith that brings salvation to our country" (Langer, 1972, p. 64). At the Nuremberg rally of September 1937, the inscription below a giant photograph of Hitler read, "In the beginning was the Word ..." the opening line of the Gospel of John. On another occasion, a photographic portrait of Hitler surrounded by a halo appeared in the front window of each of the large art shops on the Unter den Linden in Berlin (Langer, 1972, p. 64).

Other political leaders, including those in democratic countries, also sometimes need "cronies" or special people who are given unspoken tasks to become a "glass bubble" around the leader. Such "cronies" or special people see that the leader's grandiose self is safe and impenetrable. What became known as the "Nixon Method" of presidency reflected a "glass bubble" syndrome. Some individuals in Nixon's entourage such as H. Robert Haldeman and John Ehrlichman developed functions above and beyond their actual political duties in response to Nixon's need for splendid isolation. It is no wonder they were nicknamed the "Berlin Wall" surrounding the leader's lonely internal kingdom.

We can ask if Donald Trump's firing of several persons who were around him had anything to do with his attempt to keep his "glass bubble" functional. We can also ask if his obsession with building a wall is linked to a "glass bubble" fantasy.

Peculiarities in language and reality blurring

Individuals with narcissistic personality who sought treatment with members of the Charlottesville Psychoanalytic Study Group divided others into their adorers or not adorers. They obsessively referred to the first group of people by using words such as "fantastic," "incredible," "unbelievable," or "excellent," and to the second group as "fake," "overrated," "stupid," or "ignorant." Our patients tried to remove averageness by collecting real or fantasized glories. Lying, in order to protect grandiosity, was a "normal" behavior pattern for them.

I believe that noticing identical language peculiarities in Donald Trump's tweets and speeches (especially when they are not prepared earlier by a speech writer and then read by him) have led many Americans to think of him as someone with exaggerated narcissism. One news report stated that he tells an average of twenty-three lies a day.

Emotions

Individuals with narcissistic personality are prone to envy, greed, and rage—emotions associated with the covert hungry self, but also with threats against the grandiose self. They are envious of others with greater self-esteem or possessions as if others stole what they were entitled to. These patients also experience rage toward others when their own grandiose selves are threatened. If they cannot easily deny and escape the reality that their "competitor" may have superior power, beauty, or intelligence, they will develop paranoid-like ideation or experience shame and humiliation.

Additionally, individuals with narcissistic personality do not fully develop or express certain emotions. The psychoanalyst will witness this when the patient with such personality is on the couch. Prominent among feelings that such patients will not show are sorrow, remorse, and gratitude. These are feelings that relate to caring for others, depending on them, and not wanting to devalue them. Patients holding on to their grandiose selves do not use such emotions. Many individuals perceived Donald Trump as having no sorrow and empathy when he threw paper towels to people in Puerto Rico after the devastating hurricane.

Apple pie metaphor

In 2004 I provided the metaphor of a baked apple pie to illustrate the internal map of narcissistic leaders' personality and the psychodynamics of processes that make them reparative, destructive, or both (Volkan, 2004). Let us imagine that while placing the pie on the dinner table, a bottle of salad dressing spills and soaks a small section of the pie. To protect the edible and larger section of the pie, we cut off the spoiled section and push it to the periphery of the serving plate. The large, edible piece symbolizes the portion of the narcissistic leader's grandiose self; the smaller, spoiled piece stands for the individual's devalued self and object images (hungry self). Because people with narcissistic personality are unable to integrate the inflated, grandiose part of themselves with the devalued, humiliated aspects, it becomes essential that the "good" piece not touch the "spoiled" piece (splitting).

A political leader with a narcissistic personality applies various ego tasks to deal with the spoiled piece of pie, as it reflects in the leader's political decision-making, leader–followers or leader–"enemy" inter-actions, and historical processes. Dealing with the spoiled piece of pie in one way makes the leader with a narcissistic personality "reparative." Returning to our apple pie metaphor, the reparative leader tries to wipe the salad dressing from the spoiled piece or attempts to sweeten it and improve it enough to allow it to remain on the same plate as the unspoiled piece and perhaps even to touch it. Such a leader wishes for his or her followers to achieve an imagined and hoped-for high level of functioning to reflect the leader's shining self-image and be extensions of his or her superiority. The opposite of a reparative narcissistic leader is one who is determined to destroy the spoiled piece of pie. For this leader, a destructive one, it may not be enough to push the spoiled piece of pie further away from the good piece on the same plate or even "externalize" it onto another plate. The spoiled piece of pie has to be destroyed.

The founder of modern Turkey, Kemal Atatürk, saw himself as above others—and his followers perceived him as such. He did not, however, seek fantasized enemies or subgroups to devalue or destroy in order to remain superior. His narcissism expressed itself quite differently:

> Why, after my years of education, after studying civilizations and the socializing processes, should I descend to the level of common people? I will make them rise to my level. Let me not resemble them; they should resemble me. (Aydemir, 1969, p. 482)

Atatürk became one of the best examples of reparative leaders.

Let us go back to Adolf Hitler. We can imagine that even he showed some reparative qualities. Nazis themselves, in Judith Stern's terms, were made into "small gods" by their imitation of Hitler (Stern, 2001). In a sense, Hitler attempted to enhance the self-esteem of his followers. But, as a malignant narcissist, this reparative activity could only take place at the expense of other groups that were dehumanized and destroyed. Those followers that were made "little gods" were not actually given their personal "freedoms," but were used to enforce the leader's "glass bubble."

Last words

As every schoolchild knows each century lasts 100 years, but just when each century starts and ends is entirely another matter. Arguments could be made for combining the nineteenth and twentieth centuries, wherever you start and end them, whether in 1789 or 1815 to 1914 or to 1950, into a single time period under the old rubric of the Age of Nationalism. Or, we could call our nineteenth century, whatever its delimitations might be, the Age of Nationalism: Part I, and the twentieth century, again, whatever its dates might be, the Age of Nationalism: Part II. For the twenty-first century, from wherever you want to start it, for example, from the retreat of the British, French, and Dutch empires, or the collapse of the Soviet Union, to whenever, ethnicity is making a strong claim right now to morph itself into what my late historian friend and coauthor of four books Norman Itzkowitz called the Age of Ethnicity. Itzkowitz did not mean to say that ethnicity has just emerged as a virulent element in relations among peoples. We need not go back too far into history to find significant examples of the role played by ethnicity in the unfolding of historical situations. It would certainly be amiss not to recognize the role of ethnicity in Oliver Cromwell's conquest of Ireland, and equally wrong-headed not to see the subsequent impact of that ethnic conflict in the New World. Many of the leading colonists, such as John Smith who had a key role in the establishment of the first English settlement in American, had their baptism of fire in the conquest of Ireland. They brought the lessons of that ethnic conflict with them. For them, the indigenous populations were often the Irish in other guises.

In this book I refer to incredible advances in communication and travel technologies, DNA tests, robots, expanded financial markets beyond national borders, voluntary and forced immigration, refugee crises, terrorism, and using tweets for propaganda and diplomacy. These events have contributed to the globalization of the metaphorical question "Who are we now?" I suggested that now we are experiencing a "Who are we now civilization." Despite efforts to bury it, large-group identity—certainly ethnic identity, but also national, religious, and ideological ones—has been and is still here, and will continue to be here into the foreseeable future.

Let me go back to May 2006 when the focus was on "togetherness" in Europe. I gave a keynote speech at the European Association of Transcultural Group Analysis (EATGA) in Budapest, Hungary on May 25. The organizers of this meeting had what I call an "experiment" that illustrated the power of large-group identity when it pitched against the Other's large-group identity. Participants to this meeting had come from various European countries such as Hungary, Austria, the United Kingdom, Italy, and France which were already full members of the European Union (EU) as well from the Eastern European countries such as Croatia, Serbia, and Romania which, at that time were aspiring to be full members of the EU.

The participants were divided into groups of ten people and they were given a task to speak about their perceptions of the EU and to describe the contributions of their own countries to the EU. In other words, members of each small group were given a direct or indirect task to be a spokesperson for his or her large group. Each small group was assigned a leader. The official accepted language for this gathering was English. The participants of one small group that I observed were all well-known professional persons in the mental health field.

They started by making references to the greatness of the EU and to its task of providing a common and idealized umbrella for many large-group identities. Within fifteen to twenty minutes the "Otherness" was perceived as a threat against each participant's primary large-group identity and emotions flared up. First, one participant started to speak in French after stating in English that under the European Union's umbrella all languages should be given equal attention and respect. The next participant started to speak in Italian and mayhem broke out.

Today Brexit is the withdrawal of the United Kingdom from the European Union. Discussions have taken place about "Grexit." There are other types of large-group identity problems in Europe, such as those in Spain, and in many other locations of the world such as the one which was illustrated by an independence referendum for Iraqi Kurdistan which was held on September 25, 2017.

At the present time, I do not have in-depth information about most large-group identity conflicts. I am very familiar with the seemingly unending ethnic problems in Cyprus, especially since I have been spending my summer months on the island for the last two decades. I follow closely the Republic of Georgia's large-group identity issues with the breakaway states of South Ossetia and Abkhazia as well as with Russia because I had gone to the Republic of Georgia many times with other members of the Center for the Study of Mind and Human Interaction (CSMHI) from 1998 to 2002 and have kept in touch with my Georgian friends since then. From 2009 to 2012 I conducted a series of unofficial dialogues between Turks and Kurds in Turkey. After each meeting I met with Abdullah Gül who was the president of Turkey at that time. Today, I watch the news about the so-called "Kurdish problem" in Turkey with sadness. In this book I described my recent unexpected involvement in finding solutions to problems on Pitcairn Island. After the president of the International Dialogue Initiative (IDI) Gerard Fromm and I, and two other members of the IDI, began offering teaching seminars I learned details of other large-group identity issues and tragedies from the participants, such as what is happening in South Sudan.

I hope that large-group psychology in its own right becomes a required course in psychoanalytic training institutes. Studying and developing large-group psychology *in its own right* is a necessity in order for psycho-analysts to have a serious voice in national and world affairs. I also wish that there will be a serious interest within the official diplomatic world to consider the benefits from the contributions of large-group psychology for evolving a more peaceful world.

Addendum: COVID-19, psychoanalysis, and large-group psychology

onald Trump's remarks about the events in Charlottesville, Virginia, which took place on August 11–12, 2017 motivated me to write this book. These remarks were perceived as an accoutrement for societal division. An examination of the causes of such divisions became a focus of this book which I wrote during the summer of 2019 while in North Cyprus.

The impeachment of President Donald Trump occurred on December 18, 2019. The United States House of Representatives approved articles of impeachment on charges of abuse of power and obstruction of Congress. The Senate acquitted Donald Trump at the end of his impeachment trial on February 5, 2020. His acquittal was almost unanimously on political party lines. We witnessed the deepening political division in the United States. During this period Donald Trump once more reflected the character of his personality organization.

As the final editing of the book was underway, the global outbreak of COVID-19 became an unexpected "enemy" for humankind. During the first week of March 2020, I was in Vilnius as a guest of the Lithuanian Ministry of Foreign Affairs. I participated in an international meeting which was part of Lithuania's celebration of the thirtieth anniversary of its secession from the Soviet Union. My interdisciplinary team from the University of Virginia's Center for the Study and Human Interaction (CSMHI) and I had first gone to Lithuania in April 1992. At that time, we met with representatives of the Lithuanian government and then facilitated a meeting with participants from Lithuania, Latvia, Estonia and the Soviet

Union. This was the beginning of our seven years work in the Baltic states, mostly in Estonia. We tried to provide help and support for the Baltic states in their efforts to restore their independence in a peaceful fashion. As March 2020 approached, I was aware of the danger of getting contaminated with the corona virus especially through travel. But memories of our work in Lithuania and the other Baltic states made me to deny this danger. I wanted to take part in this government-sponsored meeting. I was also excited that the meeting organizers wanted this gathering to be "a marriage between diplomacy and psychoanalysis."

The meeting was opened by the former Lithuanian President Valdas Adamkus and was attended by well-known scholars, diplomats, and artists from Lithuania as well as other countries. The Lithuanians remembered the individual and societal traumas of their undigested Soviet past. I could easily hear their continuing fear of Russia. This meeting also opened a door for Lithuania to examine what had happened to the Lithuanian Jews in 1941. In that period of time there were approximately 250,000 Jews in Lithuania, or 10% of the total population. During the German invasion 206,800 of them were murdered by the Nazis and Lithuanian collaborators.

While I was in Lithuania, social distancing did not seem to be in the minds of people at the meeting, open markets, and in the streets. On my way back to the United States, I had to change airplanes and had to wait at the Amsterdam International Airport for four hours. I lost my denial mechanism in this crowded environment. After coming home to the United States, I noticed that for the first fourteen days I was checking to see if I might have any COVID-19 symptoms. Then I began collecting observations on the impact of the corona virus pandemic on individuals and large groups.

After the spread of COVID-19, the International Psychanalytical Association (IPA) and other psychoanalytic associations provided guidelines for distance treatment by taking advantage of phone or online technologies. At the present time, I am supervising the therapeutic cases of nine younger psychoanalysts in different countries. I know in detail the life stories and internal worlds of the sixteen patients they are treating. Some patients began lying on a couch in their homes. They would only see via the internet the analyst at the beginning and the end of their sessions and talk to the analyst and hear him or her during the rest of the therapeutic session.

It is beyond the scope of this book to give detailed examples of the *initial* impact of the virus pandemic on individuals behind observable denial, fear, anxiety, and devastating pain. I only wish to share some of my observations on how the sixteen analysands have responded to the pandemic and social distancing from their psychoanalysts. They returned, consciously and unconsciously, to their childhood losses and re-experienced anxieties and old defense mechanisms and fantasies linked to such losses.

Five middle-aged patients expressed open anger towards older people in their environments and in their cities. During their early childhood these five individuals had not received good parenting. They had experienced open and hidden guilt feelings due to their rage against their parents. During their analyses they were having a difficult time with letting their murderous fantasies surface. Now they could openly express their murderous rage against the older people who represented their parental figures because they would not be actual murderers, COVID-19 would be the killer. They would be saved then from feeling guilty.

I also observed how a massive shared threat on an individual's well-being could connect with this individual's large-group history. A man in his early thirties had been in analysis for four years when COVID-19 became a pandemic. He and his ancestors are members of a rather small Jewish community in a country where they were not directly affected by the Holocaust. During the first telecommunication session with his analyst, he filled the hour by referring to his identification with Anne Frank. He felt that, by not being able to come to his analyst's office, he was forced to go into hiding, like Anne Frank had done. At home he became preoccupied with the news of the virus situation in Israel.

Psychoanalysts themselves, staying alone in their offices or at another private location while continuing to work with their analysands via computer began to seek support for their own loneliness. For example, one psychoanalyst noticed two pigeons on his balcony. He started feeding them. Then he built a nest for them and began to keep his door to the balcony open. Within two weeks these two birds began entering into his office, eating bird food on the psychoanalyst's desk while he was conducting distant psychoanalysis. I must add that one of his patients while lying on a couch at home for her treatment away from her family members began holding on her cat tightly on her home couch. I also realized how I, as the supervisor, was required to be very careful to remain as a non-anxious, steady object for my supervisees.

Now let us look at the *initial* societal/political responses to the COVID-19 pandemic. As I listen to the coronavirus news updates, I realize how they are closely linked to themes that appear in this book. How border psychology, societal divisions, racist attitudes, and expectations from political leaders have become the primary preoccupations of large groups along with medical, economic, and other realistic issues. Let us examine this by looking briefly at different types of major shared catastrophes.

Some massive traumas are from earthquakes, tropical storms, floods, forest fires, volcanic eruptions, and other natural causes. When nature shows its fury and people suffer, those affected tend ultimately to accept the event as fate or as the will of God. Following man-made accidental disasters, survivors blame a small number of individuals for their carelessness. Both natural and accidental catastrophes usually do not bring ethnic, national, or religious border issues to our minds, unless the second-type disaster is like the 1986 Chernobyl accident that spewed tons of radioactive dust into the atmosphere. Sometimes, murdering a "transference figure" for the members of the large group, such as John F. Kennedy in the USA, Yitzhak Rabin in Israel, Olof Palme in Sweden, Giorgi Chanturia in the Republic of Georgia, and Rafik Hariri in Lebanon, provokes traumatic societal responses. When the murderer and the murdered leader belong to the same large-group identity there is no impact on border psychology.

Other massive traumas are due to the *deliberate* actions of an enemy group, as in ethnic, national, religious and political ideological conflicts, racism, terrorism, wars, and genocides. Earlier in this book, I wrote that only some massive traumas at the hand of the Other may evolve as a chosen trauma. However, all deliberately induced social traumas by the Other inflame large-group identity issues and border psychology as soon as they occur. The protection and the maintenance of the metaphorical large-group tent's canvas becomes a shared preoccupation.

In Chapter Eight, I wrote about a fantasy of Martians coming to Earth and forcing human beings from different races and ethnic and religious backgrounds to come together against a common enemy. As a non-visible enemy, COVID-19 did not come from Mars. But like the imaginary Martians, it threatens all human beings: old people, young people, rich people, poor people, famous people, and refugees. This threat right away initiated a need to protect physical borders between countries and some locations within the same country. Since every large group needs to protect itself this was an expected and realistic development. This development, however, became linked to leader–follower psychology, large-group identity, and political themes. Donald Trump's usage of the term "Chinese virus" is an example of this. Increased attention to the physical borders and social distancing also created societal divisions and racist attitudes within the same country, such as between old persons and young persons, and white persons and persons who appeared of Asian ancestry.

Interestingly, incredible communication technology has begun to create increasing psychological "holes" in the physical borders. For example, I began receiving email message from individuals whom I had met in many countries and who, in normal times, were not in contact with me. Sharing the same "enemy," I sensed, had brought us together again. I received an invitation from China to give a Zoom seminar to mental health workers on social trauma, loss, and mourning. I willingly did that on April 3, 2020. I was informed that 8,000 individuals listened to me. When my seminar ended there was time to receive questions from the listeners. I noted that the first question they asked me was not a medical one. They wanted to know why Donald Trump had referred COVID-19 as the "Chinese virus." I noted large-group identity concern was a prominent concern.

In Chapter Six, I wrote how the International Dialogue Initiative (IDI) meetings, have become a symbol for me illustrating the importance of psychologically informed dialogues in removing irrational views of one another and opening a reflective space of communication among people with different large-group identities. On April 5, 2020, members of the IDI had their first telecommunication gathering under the leadership of the IDI President Gerard Fromm. Our member from Palestine could not join us due to technical problems. The other twenty-two members from seven different counties shared their personal experiences, the nature of the anxieties related to business, the impact of the grieving process and its rituals, and the anger at betrayal by incompetent persons in authority. Listening to other members of the IDI, I also noted once more concerns about large-group identity and societal divisions, especially those supported by organized religions. We noted that deep denial over COVID-19's danger by some local religious leaders and religious organizations is taking place worldwide. The day after our first IDI telecommunication gathering, I heard from a colleague in the Republic of Georgia. She described the political reasons why the government was not daring to interfere with the Orthodox Church. Church members were continuing to have wine from one shared spoon and kiss the same cross.

Since Donald Trump's remarks about the events in Charlottesville on August 11–12, 2017 motivated me to write this book, I will finish my

Addendum by noticing how his language pattern at the present time, in April 2020, continues to stimulate societal division in the USA. During his daily virus briefings, the words "incredible" and "fantastic" are heard again and again. Sometimes within a minute he mentions "incredible" three times. Almost all of his themes connected with this word refers to his and his followers "greatness." Meanwhile, he continues, during almost every briefing, to verbally devalue those who question his sense of superiority.

By looking back at deadly plagues throughout history, such as the Black Death peaking in Europe and causing the deaths of 75–200 million people in Eurasia and North Africa in the fourteenth century, some scholars expect huge social, economic, and technological changes after the COVID-19 pandemic is over. We will have to wait to evaluate from a psychological point of view how this "enemy" will influence large-group psychology and international relationships.

April 16, 2020

References

Abse, D. W., & Jessner, L. (1961). The psychodynamic aspect of leadership. *Daedalus, 90*: 693–710.

Achen, C. H., & Snidal, D. (1989). Rational deterrence theory and comparative case studies. *World Politics, 41*: 143–169.

Adams, M. V. (1996). *The Multicultural Imagination: "Race", Color, and the Unconscious.* London: Routledge.

Ainslie, R. C., & Solyom, A. E. (1986). The replacement of fantasied oedipal child: A disruptive effect of sibling loss on the mother-child relationship. *Psychoanalytic Psychology, 3*: 257–268.

Akhtar, S. (1992). *Broken Structures: Severe Personality Disorders and Their Treatment.* Northvale, NJ: Jason Aronson.

Akhtar, S. (1999). *Immigration and Identity: Turmoil, Treatment, Transformation.* Northvale, NJ: Jason Aronson.

Allison, G. T. (1971). *The Essence of Decision: Explaining the Cuban Missile Crisis.* Boston, MA: Little Brown.

Andrews, S. C., & Fenton, J. P. (2001). Archeology and the invisible man: the role of slavery in the production of wealth and social class in the Bluegrass region of Kentucky, 1820 to 1870. *World Archeology, 33*: 115.

Anzieu, D. (1971). L'illusion groupale. *Nouvelle Revue de Psychânalyse, 4*: 73–93.

Anzieu, D. (1984). *The Group and the Unconscious.* London: Routledge & Kegan Paul.

Apprey, M. (1996). Broken lines, public memory, absent memory: Jewish and African Americans coming to grips with racism. *Mind and Human Interaction, 7*: 139–149.

Apprey, M. (1998). Reinventing the self in the face of received transgenerational hatred in the African American community. *Mind and Human Interaction, 9*: 30–37.

Arıboğan, D. U. (2018). *Duvar: Tarih Geri Dönüyor* [*Wall: History is Repeating*]. Istanbul: İnkilap.

Arnett, J. J. (2002). The psychology of globalization. *American Psychologist, 37*: 774–783.

Atik, F. (2019). *A Psychoanalyst on His Own Couch: A Biography of Vamık Volkan and His Psychoanalytic and Psychopolitical Concepts*. London: Phoenix.

Aydemir, Ş. S. (1969). *Tek Adam* [The Singular Man], *Vol. 3*. Istanbul: Remzi Kitabevi.

Barner-Barry, C., & Rosenwein, R. (1985). *Psychological Perspectives of Politics*. Engelwood Cliffs, NJ: Prentice-Hall.

Baysal, E., Indrak, K., Bozkurt, G., Berkalp, A., Aritkan, E., Old, J. M., Ioannou, P., Angastiniotis, M., Yüregir, G. T., Kılınç, Y., & Huisman, T. H. J. (1992). The β-thalassaemia mutations in the population of Cyprus. *British Journal of Haemathology, 81*: 607–609.

Bernard, W. W., Ottenberg, P., & Redl, F. (1973). Dehumanization: A composite psychological defense in relation to modern war. In: N. Sanford & C. Comstock (Eds.), *Sanctions for Evil: Sources of Social Destructiveness* (pp. 102–124). San Francisco, CA Adams, M. V. (1996). *The Multicultural Imagination: "Race", Color, and the Unconscious*. London: Routledge: Jossey-Bass.

Bloom, P. (2010). *How Pleasure Works: The New Science of Why We Like What We Like*. New York: W. W. Norton.

Blos, P. (1962). *On Adolescence*. New York: Free Press.

Blos, P. (1967). The second individuation process of adolescence. *Psychoanalytic Study of the Child, 22*: 162–186.

Boyer, L. B. (1986). One man's need to have enemies: A psychoanalytic perspective. *Journal of Psychoanalytic Anthropology, 9*: 101–120.

Brenner, I. (2014). *Dark Matters: Exploring the Realm of Psychic Devastation*. London: Karnac.

Brenner, I. (Ed.) (2019). *The Handbook of Psychoanalytic Holocaust Studies: International Perspectives*. New York: Routledge.

Brody, E. B. (1963). Color and identity conflict in young boys. *Psychiatry, 26*: 188–201.

Burns, J. M. (1984). *The Power to Lead: Crises of the American Presidency*. New York: Simon & Schuster.

Cain, A. C., & Cain, R. C. (1964). On replacing a child. *Journal of the American Academy of Child Psychiatry, 3*: 443–456.

Cann, R. L., Stoneking, M., & Wilson, A. C. (1987). Mitochondrial DNA and human evolution. *Nature, 3*: 31–36.

Çevik, A. (2003). Globalization and identity. In: S. Varvin & V. D. Volkan (Eds.), *Violence or Dialogue: Psychoanalytic Insights to Terror and Terrorism* (pp. 91–98). London: International Psychoanalysis Library.

Chakotin, S. (1939). *The Rape of the Masses: The Psychology of Totalitarian Political Propaganda.* New York: Haskell House, 1971.

Charles, C. V. (1942). Optimism and frustration in the American Negro. *Psychoanalytic Review, 29*: 270.

Chasseguet-Smirgel, J. (1984). *The Ego Ideal.* New York: W. W. Norton.

Dai, B. (1953). Some problems of personality development among Negro children. In: C. Kluckhohn & H. A. Murray (Eds.), *Personality in Nature, Society and Culture* (pp. 565–566). New York: Alfred A. Knopf.

D'Antonio, M. (2016). *The Truth About Trump.* New York: St. Martin's Press.

Davis, K. (2019). Digital archive traces admissions to country's first mental hospital for Blacks. *Psychiatric News, 54*(8): 10–12.

Emde, R. (1991). Positive emotions for psychoanalytic theory: Surprises from infancy research and new directions. *Journal of the American Psychoanalytic Association* (Supplement) *39*: 5–44.

Erikson, E. H. (1956). The problem of ego identity. *Journal of the American Psychoanalytic Association, 4*: 56–121.

Erikson, E. H. (1985). *Childhood and Society.* New York: W. W. Norton.

Faimberg, H. (2005). *The Telescoping of Generations: Listening to the Narcissistic Links Between Generations.* London: Routledge.

Fogel, R. W., & Engerman, S. L. (1995). *Time on the Cross: The Economics of American Negro Slavery.* New York: W. W. Norton.

Follett, R. (2003). Heat, sex, and sugar: Pregnancy and childbearing in the slave quarters. *Journal of Family History, 28*: 510–539.

Foulkes, E. (1973). *S. H. Foulkes: Selected Papers.* London: Karnac.

Freud, A., & Burlingham, D. (1942). *War and Children.* New York: International Universities Press.

Freud, S. (1905d). *Three Essays on the Theory of Sexuality. S. E., 7*: 130–242. London: Hogarth.

Freud, S. (1912–13). *Totem and Taboo. S. E., 13*: 1–164. London: Hogarth.

Freud, S. (1917e). Mourning and melancholia. *S. E., 14*: 237–260. London: Hogarth.

Freud, S. (1918a). The taboo of virginity. *S. E., 11*: 191–208. London: Hogarth.

Freud, S. (1921c). *Group Psychology and the Analysis of the Ego. S. E., 18*: 67–143. London: Hogarth.

Freud, S (1926d). *Inhibitions, Symptoms, and Anxiety. S. E., 20*: 77–174. London: Hogarth.

Freud, S. (1930a). *Civilization and Its Discontents. S. E., 21*: 64–145. London: Hogarth.

Freud, S. (1933b). *Why War? S. E., 22*: 197–215. London: Hogarth.

Freud, S. (1940a). *An Outline of Psycho-Analysis. S. E., 23*: 211–253. London: Hogarth.

Friedman, R. (2008). Dream telling as a request for containment—three uses of dreams in group therapy. *International Journal of Group Psychotherapy, 58*: 327–344.

Furman. R. (1998). The pilgrims: Myth and reality. *Mind and Human Interaction, 9*: 5–17.

Goodman, M. E. (1952). *Race Awareness in Young Children*. Cambridge, MA: Addison-Wesley.

Green, N., & Solnit, A. (1964). Reactions to the threatened loss of a child: A vulnerable child syndrome. *Pediatrics, 34*: 58–66.

Greenacre, P. (1969). The fetish and the transitional object. In: *Emotional Growth, Vol. 1* (pp. 315–334). New York: International Universities Press.

Greenspan, S. (1989). *The Development of the Ego: Implications for Personality Theory, Psychopathology and Psychotherapeutic Process*. Madison, CT: International Universities Press.

Halperin, C. J. (2009). *The Tatar Yoke: The Image of the Mongols in Medieval Russia*. Bloomington, IN: Slavica.

Harari, Y. N. (2014). *Sapiens: A Brief History of Humankind*. London: Vintage.

Herzfeld, M. (1986). *Ours Once More: Folklore, Ideology, and the Making of Modern Greece*. New York: Pella.

Hitler, A. (1927). *Mein Kampf*. Boston, MA: Houghton Mifflin, 1962.

Hopper, E., & Weinberg, H. (Eds.) (2011). *The Social Unconscious in Persons, Groups, and Societies. Vol. 1: Mainly Theory*. London: Karnac.

Horowitz, D. L. (1985). *Ethnic Groups in Conflict*. Berkeley, CA: University of California Press.

Jacobson, E. (1964). *The Self and the Object World*. New York: International Universities Press.

Janis, I. L., & Mann, I. (1977). *Decision-making: A Psychological Analysis of Conflicts, Choice, and Commitment*. New York: Free Press.

Jervis, R., Lebow, N., & Stein, J. (Eds.) (1985). *Psychology of Deterrence*. Baltimore, MD: Johns Hopkins University Press.

Jowett, G. S., & O'Donnell, V. (1992). *Propaganda and Persuasion*. New York: Sage.

Jurcevic, S., & Urlic, I. (2001). Linking objects in the process of mourning for sons disappeared in war: Croatia 2001. *Croatian Medical Journal, 43*: 234–239.

Kakar, S. (1996). *The Colors of Violence: Cultural Identities, Religion, and Conflict*. Chicago, IL: University of Chicago Press.

Kennedy, J. A. (1952). Problems posed in the analysis of Negro patients. *Psychiatry, 15*: 313–327.

Kernberg, O. F. (1975). *Borderline Conditions and Pathological Narcissism*. New York: Jason Aronson.

Kernberg, O. F. (1976). *Object Relations Theory and Clinical Psychoanalysis*. New York: Jason Aronson.

Kernberg, O. F. (1980). *Internal World and External Reality: Object Relations Theory Applied*. New York: Jason Aronson.

Kernberg, O. F. (1989). Mass psychology through the analytic lens. Paper presented at Through the Looking Glass: Freud's Impact on Contemporary Culture meeting, Philadelphia, September 23.

Kernberg, O. F. (2003a). Sanctioned political violence: A psychoanalytic view— Part 1. *International Journal of Psychoanalysis, 84*: 683–698.

Kernberg, O. F. (2003b). Sanctioned political violence: A psychoanalytic view—Part 2. *International Journal of Psychoanalysis, 84*: 953–968.

Kestenberg, J. S. (1982). A psychological assessment based on analysis of a survivor's child. In: M. S. Bergman & M. E. Jucovy (Eds.), *Generations of the Holocaust* (pp. 158–177). New York: Columbia University Press.

Kinnvall, C. (2004). Globalization and religious nationalism: Self, identity, and the search for ontological security. *Political Psychology, 25*: 741–767.

Klein, M. (1946). Notes on some schizoid mechanisms. In: J. Riviere (Ed.), *Development of Psychoanalysis* (pp. 292–320). London: Hogarth.

Kogan, I. (1995). *The Cry of Mute Children: A Psychoanalytic Perspective of the Second Generation of the Holocaust*. London: Free Association.

Kohut, H. (1966). Forms and transformations of narcissism. *Journal of the American Psychoanalytic Association, 14*: 243–272.

Kohut, H. (1971). *The Analysis of the Self: A Systematic Approach to the Psychoanalytic Treatment of Narcissistic Personality Disorders*. New York: International Universities Press.

Kohut, H. (1977). *Restoration of the Self*. New York: International Universities Press.

Kris, E. (1943). Some problems of war propaganda: A note on propaganda new and old. *Psychoanalytic Quarterly, 12*: 381–399.

Langer, W. C. (1972). *The Mind of Adolf Hitler: The Secret Wartime Report*. New York: Basic Books.

Lasswell, H. D. (1938). Foreword. In: G. G. Bruntz (Ed.), *Allied Propaganda and the Collapse of the German Empire in 1918* (pp. v-viii). Stanford, CA: Stanford University Press.

Laub, D., & Podell, D. (1997). Psychoanalytic listening to historical trauma: The conflict of knowing and the imperative act. *Mind and Human Interaction, 8*: 245–260.

Le Bon, G. (1895). *The Crowd: A Study of the Popular Mind*. Mineola, NY: Dover, 2002.

Legg, C., & Sherick, I. (1976). The replacement child: A developmental tragedy. *Child Psychiatry and Human Development, 7*: 79–97.

Lehtonen, J. (2003). The dream between neuroscience and psychoanalysis: Has feeding an infant impact on brain function and the capacity to create dream images in infants? *Psychoanalysis in Europe, 57*: 175–182.

Lewis, B. (2000). Propaganda in the Middle East. Paper presented at the International Conference in Commemoration of the 78th Birthday of Yitzhak Rabin: *Patterns of political discourse: propaganda, incitement and freedom of speech*, February 29.

Lind, J. E. (1914a). The dream as a simple wish-fulfillment in the Negro. *Psychoanalytic Review*, 1: 295-300.

Lind, J. E. (1914b). The color complex in the Negro. *Psychoanalytic Review*, 1: 404–414.

Loewenberg, P. (1995). *Fantasy and Reality in History*. London: Oxford University Press.

Luke, H. (1952). *The Ottoman Province—The British Colony—1571–1948, Vol. IV*. Cambridge: Cambridge University Press.

Mahler, M. S. (1968). *On Human Symbiosis and the Vicissitudes of Individuation*. New York: International Universities Press.

Mahler, M. S., Pine, F., & Bergman, A. (1975). *The Psychological Birth of the Human Infant*. New York: Basic Books.

Markides, K. C. (1977). *The Rise and Fall of the Cyprus Republic*. New Haven, CT: Yale University Press.

Mazo, E., & Hess, S. (1967). *Nixon: A Political Portrait*. New York: Popular Library.

McDonald, M. (1970). *Not by the Color of Their Skin*. New York: International Universities Press.

Mitscherlich, A. (1971). Psychoanalysis and aggression of large groups. *International Journal of Psychoanalysis, 52*: 161–167.

Modell, A. H. (1975). A narcissistic defense against affects and the illusion of self-sufficiency. *International Journal of Psychoanalysis, 56*: 275–282.

Moses, R. (1990). On dehumanizing the enemy. In: V. D. Volkan, D. A. Julius, & J. V. Montville (Eds.), *The Psychodynamics of International Relations, Vol. 1*. Lexington, MA: Lexington.

Murphy, R. F. (1957). Ingroup hostility and social cohesion. *American Anthropologist, 59*: 1018–1035.

Myers, H. J., & Yochelson, L. (1948). Color denial in the Negro. *Psychiatry, 11*: 39–46.

Niederland, W. G. (1961). The problem of the survivor. *Journal of the Hillside Hospital, 10*: 233-247.

Niederland, W. G. (1968). Clinical observations of the "Survivor Syndrome." *International Journal of Psychoanalysis, 49*: 313-315.

Ohlmeier, D. (1991). The return of the repressed: Psychoanalytical reflections on the unification of Germany. Paper presented to the Sandor Ferenczi Society, Budapest, June 7.

Olinick, S. L. (1980). *The Psychotherapeutic Instrument*. New York: Jason Aronson.

Parens, H. (1979). *The Development of Aggression in Childhood*. New York: Jason Aronson.

Pinderhughes, C. A. (1969). The origins of racism. *International Journal of Psychiatry, 8*: 934–941.

Pines, M., & Lipgar, R. (Eds.) (2002). *Building on Bion*. London: Jessica Kingsley.

Poznanski, E. O. (1972). The "replacement child": A saga of unresolved parental grief. *Behavioral Pediatrics, 81*: 1190–1193.

Prince, R. M. (2018). The lonely passion of the "people." *American Journal of Psychoanalysis, 78*: 445–462.

Purhonen, M., Kilpeläinen-Lees, R., Valkonen-Korhonen, M., Karhu, J., & Lehtonen, J. (2005). Four-month-old infants process own mother's voice faster than unfamiliar voices: Electrical signs of sensitization in infant brain. *Cognitive Brain Research, 3*: 627–633.

Rangell, L. (1971). The decision-making process: A contribution from psychoanalysis. *Psychoanalytic Study of the Child, 26*: 425–452.

Rangell, L. (1980). *The Mind of Watergate*. New York: W. W. Norton.

Reimann, V. (1976). *Goebbels: The Man Who Created Hitler*. S. Wendt (Trans.). New York: Doubleday.

Reisman, A. (2006). *Turkey's Modernization: Refugees from Nazism and Atatürk's Vision*. Washington, DC: New Academia.

Reppen, J. (Ed.) (1985). *Analysts at Work: Practice, Principles and Techniques*. Hillsdale, NJ: The Analytic Press.

Ritvo, S., & Solnit, A. (1958). Influences of early mother-child interactions on the identification process. *Psychoanalytic Study of the Child, 13*: 64–85.

Robben, C. G. A. (2000). The assault on basic trust: Disappearance, protest, and reburial in Argentina. In: A. C. G. Robben & M. M. Suarez-Orozco (Eds.), *Cultures Under Siege: Collective Violence and Trauma* (pp. 70–101). Cambridge: Cambridge University Press.

Rochau, A. L. von (1853). *Grundsätze der Realpolitik: ausgewendet auf die staatlichen Zustände Deutschlands*. Truro, UK: HardPress, 2018.

Rokeach, M. (1984). Belief system theory of stability and change. In: S. L. Ball-Rokeach, M. Rokeach, & J. W. Grube (Eds.), *The Great American Values Test: Influencing Behavior and Belief Through Television* (pp. 17–38). New York: Free Press.

Rosenthal, G. (1997). *Der Holocaust im Leben von drei Generationen: Familien von Überlebenden der Shoah und von Nazi-Tätern* [Holocaust in the Life of Three Generations: Families of Survivors of Shoah and Nazi Perpetrators]. Giessen, Germany: Psychosozial-Verlag.

Schützenberger, A. A. (1998). *The Ancestor Syndrome: Transgenerational Psychotherapy and the Hidden Links in the Family Tree*. New York: Routledge.

Šebek, M. (1996). The fate of the totalitarian object. *International Forum of Psychoanalysis, 5*: 289–294.

Sells, M. A. (2002). The construction of Islam in Serbian religious mythology and its consequences. In: M. Schatzmiller (Ed.), *Islam and Bosnia* (pp. 56–85). Montreal, Canada: McGill University Press.

Shengold, L. (1991). *Soul Murder: The Effects of Childhood Abuse and Deprivation*. New York: Ballantine.

Simmons, M. (2015). *The British and Cyprus*. Stroud, UK: The History Press.

Spitz, R. (1965). *The First Year of Life*. New York: International Universities Press.

Stapley, L. (2006). *Globalization and Terrorism: Death of a Way of Life*. London: Karnac.

Stein, J. (1988). Building politics into psychology: The misperception of threat. *Political Psychology, 9*: 245–271.

Stern, D. N. (1985). *The Interpersonal World of the Infant: A View from Psychoanalysis and Developmental Psychology*. New York: Basic Books.

Stern, J. (2001). Deviance in the Nazi society. *Mind and Human Interaction, 12*: 218–237.

Streeck-Fischer, A. (1999). Naziskins in Germany: How traumatization deals with the past. *Mind and Human Interaction, 10*: 84–97.

Suistola, J., & Volkan, V. D. (2017). *Religious Knives: Historical and Psychological Dimensions of International Terrorism*. Durham, NC: Pitchstone.

Tähkä, V. (1984). Dealing with object loss. *Scandinavian Psychoanalytic Review, 7*: 13–33.

Thomson, J. A., Harris, M., Volkan, V. D., & Edwards, B. (1995). The psychology of Western European neo-racism. *International Journal of Group Rights, 3*: 1–30.

Tucker, R. (1973). *Stalin as Revolutionary*. New York: W. W. Norton.

Twemlow, S., & Sacco, F. (2008). *Why School Anti-Bullying Programs Don't Work: A Guide to Improving School Climates*. New York: Routledge.

Vitols, M. M., Walters, H. G., & Keeler, M. H. (1963). Hallucinations and delusions in white and Negro schizophrenics. *American Journal of Psychiatry, 120*: 472–476.

Volkan, V. D. (1972). The "linking objects" of pathological mourners. *Archives of General Psychiatry, 27*: 215–222.

Volkan, V. D. (1976). *Primitive Internalized Object Relations: A Clinical Study of Schizophrenic, Borderline and Narcissistic Patients*. New York: International Universities Press.

Volkan, V. D. (1979a). *Cyprus—War and Adaptation: A Psychoanalytic History of Two Ethnic Groups in Conflict*. Charlottesville, VA: University of Virginia Press.

Volkan, V. D. (1979b). The glass bubble of a narcissistic patient. In: J. LeBoit & A. Capponi (Eds.), *Advances in Psychotherapy of the Borderline Patient* (pp. 405–431). New York: Jason Aronson.

Volkan, V. D. (1980). Narcissistic personality organization and "reparative" leadership. *International Journal of Group Psychotherapy, 30*: 131–152.

Volkan, V. D. (1981). *Linking Objects and Linking Phenomena: A Study of the Forms, Symptoms, Metapsychology and Therapy of Complicated Mourning.* New York: International Universities Press.

Volkan, V. D. (1988). *The Need to Have Enemies and Allies: From Clinical Practice to International Relationships.* Northvale, NJ: Jason Aronson.

Volkan, V. D. (1991a). On "chosen trauma." *Mind and Human Interaction*, 3: 13.

Volkan, V. D. (1991b). An interview with Valentin Berezhkov: Stalin's interpreter. *Mind and Human Interaction*, 2: 77–80.

Volkan, V. D. (1992). Ethnonationalist rituals: An introduction. *Mind and Human Interaction*, 4: 3–19.

Volkan, V. D. (1996). Bosnia-Herzegovina: Ancient fuel of a modern inferno. *Mind and Human Interaction*, 7: 110–127.

Volkan, V. D. (1997). *Bloodlines: From Ethnic Pride to Ethnic Terrorism.* New York: Farrar, Straus and Giroux.

Volkan, V. D. (1999a). The Tree Model: a comprehensive psychopolitical approach to unofficial diplomacy and the reduction of ethnic tension. *Mind and Human Interaction*, 10: 142–206.

Volkan, V. D. (1999b). Nostalgia as a linking phenomenon. *Journal of Applied Psychoanalytic Studies*, 1: 169–179.

Volkan, V. D. (1999c). *Das Versagen der Diplomatie: Zur Psychoanalyse nationaler, ethnischer und religiöser Konflikte* [The Failure of Diplomacy: The Psychoanalysis of National, Ethnic and Religious Conflicts]. Giessen, Germany: Psychosozial-Verlag.

Volkan, V. D. (1999d). Psychoanalysis and diplomacy, part two: Large-group rituals. *Journal of Applied Psychoanalytic Studies*, 1: 223–247.

Volkan, V. D. (2004). *Blind Trust: Large Groups and Their Leaders in Times of Crisis and Terror.* Charlottesville, VA: Pitchstone.

Volkan, V. D. (2006). *Killing in the Name of Identity: A Study of Bloody Conflicts.* Charlottesville, VA: Pitchstone.

Volkan, V. D. (2010). *Psychoanalytic Technique Expanded: A Textbook on Psychoanalytic Treatment.* Istanbul: Oa Press.

Volkan, V. D. (2013). *Enemies on the Couch: A Psychopolitical Journey Through War and Peace.* Durham, NC: Pitchstone.

Volkan, V. D. (2014a). *Psychoanalysis, International Relations, and Diplomacy: A Sourcebook on Large-Group Psychology.* London: Karnac.

Volkan, V. D. (2014b). Father quest and linking objects: A story of the American World War II Orphans Network (AWON) and Palestinian orphans. In: P. Cohen, M. Sossin, & R. Ruth (Eds.), *Healing in the Wake of Parental Loss: Clinical Applications and Therapeutic Strategies* (pp. 283–300). New York: Jason Aronson.

Volkan, V. D. (2016). Guns and violence in the international arena. *International Journal of Applied Psychoanalytic Studies*, 13: 102–112.

Volkan, V. D. (2017a). Preface. In: G. Leo (Ed.), *Fundamentalism and Psychoanalysis* (pp. 13–44). Lecce, Italy: Frenis Zero Press.

Volkan, V. D. (2017b). *Immigrants and Refugees: Trauma, Perennial Mourning, and Border Psychology*. London: Karnac.

Volkan, V. D. (2018a). From earthquakes to ethnic cleansing: Massive trauma and its individualized and societal consequences. In: A. Hamburger (Ed.), *Trauma, Trust, and Memory: Social Trauma and Reconciliation in Psychoanalysis, Psychotherapy, and Cultural Memory* (pp. 5–12). London: Karnac.

Volkan, V. D. (2018b). Refugees as the Other: Large-group identity, terrorism and border psychology. *Group Analysis, 51*: 343–358.

Volkan, V. D. (2018c). Mourning, large-group identity, and the refugee experience. In: T. Wenzel & B. Drozdek (Ed.), *An Uncertain Safety: Integrative Health Care for the 21st Century Refugees* (pp. 23–35). New York: Springer.

Volkan, V. D. (2019). Large-group identity, who are we now? Leader–follower relationship and societal-political divisions. *American Journal of Psychoanalysis, 79*: 139–155.

Volkan, V. D., Akhtar, S., Dorn, R. M., Kafka, J. S., Kernberg, O. F., Olsson, P. A., Rogers, R. R., & Shanfield, S. (1998). The psychodynamics of leaders and decision-making. *Mind and Human Interaction, 9*: 129–181.

Volkan, V. D., & Ast, G. (1994). *Spektrum des Narzißmus: Eine klinische Studie des gesunden Narzißmus, des Narzißtisch-masochistischen Charakters, der Narzißtischen Persönlichkeitsorganisation, des Malignen Narzißmus und des Erfolgreichen Narzißmus* [Spectrum of Narcissism: A Clinical Study of Healthy Narcissism, Narcissistic-Masochistic Character, Narcissistic Personality-Organization, Malignant Narcissism, and Successful Narcissism]. Göttingen, Germany: Vandenhoeck & Ruprecht.

Volkan, V. D., & Ast, G. (1997). *Siblings in the Unconscious and Psychopathology*. Madison, CT: International Universities Press.

Volkan, V. D., Ast, G., & Greer, W. (2002). *The Third Reich in the Unconscious: Transgenerational Transmission and Its Consequences*. New York: Brunner-Routledge.

Volkan, V. D., & Fowler, J. C. (2009). *Searching for a Perfect Woman: The Story of a Complete Psychoanalysis*. New York: Jason Aronson.

Volkan, V. D., & Itzkowitz, N. (1984). *The Immortal Atatürk: A Psychobiography*. Chicago, IL: University of Chicago Press.

Volkan, V. D., & Itzkowitz, N. (1994). *Turks and Greeks: Neighbours in Conflict*. Huntingdon, UK: Eothen Press.

Volkan, V. D., Itzkowitz, N., & Dod, A. (1997). *Richard Nixon: A Psychobiography*. New York: Columbia University Press.

Volkan, V. D., & Zintl, E. (1993). *Life After Loss: Lessons of Grief*. New York: Charles Scribner's Sons.

Waelder, R. (1936). The principle of multiple function: Observations on over-determination. *Psychoanalytic Quarterly, 5*: 45–62.

Weber, M. (1925). *Wirtschaft und Gessellschaft*. 2 vols. Tübingen, Germany: J. C. B. Mohr.

Weigert, E. (1967). Narcissism: Benign and malignant forms. In: R. W. Gibson (Ed.), *Crosscurrents in Psychiatry and Psychoanalysis* (pp. 222–238). Philadelphia, PA: Lippincott.

Werman, D. S. (1988). Freud's "narcissism of minor differences": a review and reassessment. *Journal of the American Academy of Psychoanalysis and Dynamic Psychiatry, 4*: 451–459.

Wilkerson, C. B. (1970). Destructiveness of myths. *American Journal of Psychiatry, 126*: 1087–1092.

Williams, R. M., & Parkes, C. M. (1975). Psychosocial effects of disaster: Birth rate in Aberfan. *British Medical Journal, 2*: 303–304.

Winnicott, D. W. (1953). Transitional objects and transitional phenomena. *International Journal of Psychoanalysis, 3*: 89–97.

Winnicott, D. W. (1969). Berlin walls. In: C. Winnicott, R. Shepherd, & M. Davis (Eds.), *D. W. Winnicott: Home is Where We Start From* (pp. 221–227). New York: W. W. Norton.

Yu, N., Fu, Y. X., & Li, W. H. (2002). DNA polymorphism in a worldwide sample of human x chromosomes. *Molecular Biology and Evolution, 19*: 2131–2141.

Index